Key Terms in Personnel

Steve Flinders

York Associates Publications

First published 1995

© York Associates Publications 1995

York Associates
116 Micklegate
York YO1 1JY
tel: 01904 624246
fax: 01904 646971

Printed and bound by
Quacks Books
Petergate
York YO1 2HT

ISBN 0 948333 46 4

For Lorenza

CONTENTS

INTRODUCTION

Who is the book for?

This book is for managers, employee representatives and students who want to:

1. read, understand and learn the meanings of key terms in personnel management
2. see how these terms are used so that they can use them effectively and successfully.

It is aimed primarily at people, both non-native and native speakers, who need to learn the language of personnel management. Most working people are concerned in one way or another with people management so many of these terms could be useful to almost anybody working in an organisation, not just people in personnel. The book will also be a useful source of information for Business English trainers who need to run courses in the field of personnel management for non-native speakers.

The context

The context of the book is intended to be international, although there is probably a bias towards European practice. Clearly, the personnel function is more developed in some countries than in others. While trying to avoid ideological bias, the book's underlying premise is that a company which makes a long term investment in the skills and the development of its employees will gain a long-term competitive advantage.

The definitions usually refer to "the company". This is because many users of this book will be in business. However, the terms are valid for other kinds of organisation as well - organisations in local and central government, political parties, religious organisations, etc. - in fact, any kind of organisation at all.

The language model is predominantly British English.

Organisation

The book is divided into seven chapters. Each chapter deals with an important part of personnel work. The aim is to help you to understand the basic concepts and the key terms.

Dictionaries are not usually organised in chapters. This one has been developed so that you can browse around in each area and see how terms group together. A full A-Z index comes at the end of the book.

The key terms

The terms are directly relevant to the work of personnel managers. General terms are not included, nor are very technical terms. Only in chapter 1 are more general business terms included because their understanding is important to the understanding of other more specialised terms.

The terms are defined, as far as possible, in simple language. If something is not clear, use a general dictionary.

Each entry consists of:

- a headword showing its part of speech
- the derivations from the headword
- a definition of the headword
- typical collocations
- exemplifications of the headwords

Much importance is given to collocations so that you can begin to recognize how terms really work by seeing their use in typical combinations with other words.

The exercises

Each chapter begins with a self-test so that you can check your understanding of the central concepts and key terms. Ther answers to these exercises are at the back of the book. The self-test at the beginning of each chapter consists of three exercises to test your understanding of:

- the headwords which appear in the chapter
- the defined collocations from the chapter
- additional uses of the terms from the chapter

Key to grammatical abbreviations

(n)	noun
(v)	verb
(adj)	adjective
(n ph)	noun phrase
(v ph)	verb phrase
(adj ph)	adjectival phrase

Acknowledgements

Thanks to:

- Nick Brieger for editing the text and for his suggestions about chapter organisation
- Eva Molin of Telia and Susann Hefftner of Bayer for their advice
- Trevor Toolan of Pilat for his help with "competency"
- Bill Mascull and Simon Sweeney for their encouragement.

Chapter 1

Basic Terms and Working Conditions

How many of these terms can you use?

CLOCK IN   DAY OFF   JOBLESS

HOLIDAY ENTITLEMENT   POSITION   CAPACITY

EMPLOYMENT   EMPLOYER   CONTRACT

COLLEAGUE   CONDITIONS OF EMPLOYMENT   CONSULT

DEVELOP   DIRECTOR   HOURS

COUNTERPART   DUTIES

EMPLOY   MANUAL   FLEXIBLE

WORKING   BLUE-COLLAR   DOWNGRADE   PART-TIME

LEAVE   FULL-TIME   LABOUR

GRADE   FUNCTION   HOLIDAY

MORALE   CARRY OUT   MANPOWER

PERSONNEL   HOUSE MAGAZINE   TELEWORK

HUMAN RESOURCES   JOB   HALF-TIME

SHOP FLOOR   WHITE-COLLAR   TEAM

JOB ENRICHMENT   SUBORDINATE   JOB SECURITY

PERFORM   MATERNITY LEAVE   TERMS

SEASONAL   MANPOWER PLANNING   WORK

MOTIVATE   NOTICE   OCCUPATION

TURNOVER   EMPLOYEE   SHIFT

OFF WORK   VACATION   SKILL

WORKFORCE   STAFF   SUPERIOR

SUPERVISOR   TIME OFF

Exercise 1

Complete the following sentences by deciding which of the choices A, B, C or D fits best.

1. The management proposed a new . . . . of employment with improved hours and holidays.

    A. law   B. contract   C. condition   D. capacity

2. The . . . . of a personnel manager can include recruiting new staff and negotiating with employees' representatives.

    A. duties   B. works   C. affairs   D. developments

3. The . . . . of the company have been given a 3% pay rise.

    A. staff   B. staffs   C. workforce   D. employees

4. He had a very good . . . . so everyone was surprised when he gave it up.

    A. work   B. working   C. job   D. activity

5. She works very hard so it's good that she gets paid . . . .

    A. overtime   B. full-time   C. half-time   D. part-time

6. We must . . . . the new assessment scheme before we make everyone do the interviews.

    A. fly   B. launch   C. take off   D. pilot

7.   Workers on the night . . . . in that company usually
     work from 10 at night until 6 in the morning.

     A. move   B. shift   C. group   D. assembly

8.   Staff . . . . is falling because company morale is
     improving and because the general level of unemployment is rising.

     A. turnover   B. position   C. balance   D. level

Exercise 2

Complete each of the following sentences with one of the words or phrases
from this chapter.

1.   She did not feel very well so she took a d . . . . o . . . . on
     Thursday, but she was back at work on Friday.

2.   If my company operated a f . . . . scheme, I would be
     able to take my children to school but as it is I have to start work at 8.30
     every morning.

3.   We get 25 days' paid h . . . . every year but we can
     sometimes get more unpaid h . . . . if we ask for it.

4.   He was found smoking in a no-smoking area and was told to see his
     immediate s . . . . immediately.

5.   Since the company introduced t . . . ., I have been able
     to spend almost half of my working time at home.

6

6. We used to employ large numbers of m . . . . workers but now very few of our staff work with their hands.

7. She used to work 40 hours a week but now she only works p . . . . - t . . . . so that she can spend more time with her children.

8. The company is having problems recruiting people to operate the new machinery because there is a shortage of s . . . . workers in the area.

Exercise 3

Complete each of the following sentences with one of the phrases from this chapter.

1. We needed advice that no-one in the company could give us so we had to c . . . . i . . . . . . a . . . . . . c . . . .

2. He has g . . . . o . . . . . s . . . . l . . . . because he is obviously not well.

3. When I joined this company I started on the b . . . . g . . . . and now I have reached the t . . . . g . . . .

4. We run an international m . . . . d . . . . programme which we hope gives our managers the motivation and the abilities to compete successfully anywhere in the world.

5. In times of f . . . . e . . . . , when everybody who wants a job has one, it can be sometimes be difficult to recruit people with the right level of skills.

6. The company has decided on maximum w . . . . h . . . . for the workforce so that no-one in future will be able to work more than 45 hours per week.

BLUE-COLLAR (adj phr)

A blue-collar worker is someone who works in a manual job or in a job on the factory floor. See also MANUAL, WHITE-COLLAR.

> Our company employs fewer blue-collar workers now than ten years ago because much of the production process has been automated.

CAPACITY (n)

Your capacity is your ability to learn how to do something.

* Develop one's capacity to
* Develop one's capacities

> Our aim in this company is to develop the professional capacities of all members of our staff by providing them all with at least one training course per year.

CARRY OUT (v)

When you carry out a plan or a proposal, you put it into operation.

* Carry out one's duties
* Carry out a plan
* Carry out to the letter
* Fail to carry out

> We successfully carried out the company's plan to recruit one hundred new staff before the end of the year.

CLOCK IN (v ph)

If your company wants to know the time at which you arrive at work, you have to clock in, using a CLOCK CARD or CLOCK BADGE. When you leave work, you CLOCK OUT. Alternative terms are CLOCKING ON and CLOCKING OFF.

> In the past when you inserted your clock card, the machine stamped your clock card with your arrival time mechanically, but now clocking in and out is often done electronically.

COLLEAGUE (n)

A colleague is someone who works in the same department or company or profession as you.
> I must talk to my colleagues in the department before I can tell you whether it's possible or not.

CONDITIONS OF EMPLOYMENT (n ph)

Your conditions of employment state what you have to do in your job and the rules that you and your employer must follow. These conditions are usually stated in a contract of employment. Conditions of employment can also be called CONDITIONS OF SERVICE. See also CONTRACT; Working conditions.

> Under the conditions of employment in our company, all staff have a 40 hour working week and 25 days' paid holiday per year.

CONSULT (v) consultant (n) consultative (adj) consultation (n)

When you consult someone, you ask them for their opinion or advice about something. A consultant is someone whom you pay to give you specialist or expert advice.

* Call in a consultant
* Use a consultant
* A consultative body
* A consultative committee

> The management consulted all the staff before introducing a system of flexible working hours.

CONTRACT (n) contractual (adj)

A contract is a legal agreement between two people or parties.

* A contract of employment
* An annual hours contract

> A contract of employment should deal with all the basic terms and conditions of employment such as pay, working hours, holidays, sick pay and so on.

COUNTERPART (n)

A counterpart is someone who does the same kind of job as you in another organisation.

> A counterpart visit is a good way of finding out how other people deal with the same kinds of work problems that you have.

DAY OFF (n ph)

A day off is a day when you do not go to work.

* Take a day off

> Her employer lets her take a day off now and then because she does a lot of unpaid overtime.

DEVELOP (v) development (n)

When something develops or when you develop something, it changes in a way that makes it bigger or better.

* An important development
* A significant development
* Human Resources Development
* Management development

> The personnel department is trying to develop a company health programme so that fewer working days are lost because of illness.

DIRECTOR (n) direct (v)

A director is:

1. a senior manager who works for a company full-time, for example the Managing Director, the Marketing Director, the Director of Research and Development; or
2. a person who represents the shareholders of the company on its Board of Directors.

> In our company, there are five divisional directors who meet with the Managing Director once a week.

Executive director (n ph). An executive director is a member of the Board and also a full-time manager in the company.

Non-executive director (n ph). A non-executive director is a member of the Board who comes from outside and who is not a manager in the company.

> Non-executive directors often have to decide how much the top managers of their companies should be paid.

DOWNGRADE (n, v)

If you are downgraded, you are put onto a lower grade of job. Both jobs and people can be downgraded. The opposite of downgrade is UPGRADE.

> Because of the delayering, several middle management posts have been cut and several others have been downgraded in the new organisation.

DUTIES (n pl)

Your duties are the different parts of the job that you have to do, especially for a lower grade job.

* Perform duties

> The doorman's duties include checking on everyone who enters and leaves the building.

EMPLOY (v) employee (n) employer (n) employment (n)

When you employ someone, you give him or her a job. An employer gives jobs to people. EMPLOYEES are people who work for companies. People who work for themselves are SELF-EMPLOYED. People who do not have jobs are UNEMPLOYED.

* A salaried employee
* A non-salaried employee
* Full employment
* Seasonal employment
* Employment attitude survey
* Employment law
* Employment legislation

* Employee representation
* An employers' organisation

> The company wants to employ three new sales representatives because demand for its products is growing.

Employee assistance programme (n ph). Employee assistance programmes (EAPs) offer counselling to employees with alcohol or financial or other kinds of problems.

Lifetime employment (n ph).A company offering lifetime employment guarantees jobs for its employees for the whole of their working lives.

EXEMPT (v, adj) exemption (n)

If you are exempt from a rule or a procedure, you do not have to follow it.

* exemption from liability
* exemption from contributions

> The company's security guards are exempted from the rules about parking vehicles on company property.

FLEXIBLE WORKING (n ph)

Flexible working gives employees some choice in the times when they start and finish work. Flexible working is also known as FLEXIBLE HOURS, FLEXITIME, and is called FLEXTIME in the United States.

* A flexible working week
* A flexible working year
* Flexible working hours
* Operate a flexitime scheme

> Flexible hours allowed her to take her children to school every day before starting work.

FULL-TIME (adj, adv) full-timer (n)

When you work full-time, you work the standard working week, normally about forty hours a week. A full-timer is someone who works full-time.

* Full-time employment
* On a full-time basis

> Although the total number of employees in this company is increasing, there are now fewer full-timers and more part-timers than in the past.

FUNCTION (n)

A function is a job, a position or an area of responsibility.

* The personnel function

> The function of the manpower planning officer is to make sure that the right number of people with the right skills are employed in the company at the right time.

GRADE (n)

A grade is the level of a job within the structure of a company's workforce. See also DOWNGRADE.

* A low grade
* A low grade worker
* A pay grade
* A semi-skilled grade
* A skilled grade
* An unskilled grade
* A top grade
* Move to a higher grade

> The company agreed to pay increases which would improve the position of the lower grades.

HALF-TIME (adj, adv) half-timer (n)

When you work half-time, you work half the standard working week. A half-timer is someone who works half-time.

* On a half-time basis

> Some married couples share the same job, with each partner working half-time, so that each can spend more time with their children.

HOLIDAY (n) holidays (pl n)

A holiday is a period of time when you do not have to go to work.

* Holiday money
* A holiday replacement
* National holiday
* Paid holiday
* Public holiday
* Unpaid holiday
* To be owed holiday

> The company owes her fourteen days' holiday this year because she took so little time off last year.

Holiday entitlement (n ph). Your holiday entitlement is the number of days' holiday which your contract of employment says you can take per year.

> He asked for a few days' unpaid holiday since he had already used up all his entitlement for the year.

13

HOURS (n pl)

Your hours are the length of time you spend at work per day, per week or for some other period.

* A 40-hour week
* Maximum working hours
* Work long hours

> He always has to work long hours at this time of year in order to finish the departmental budget on time.

Annual hours (n ph). If you work under a system of annual hours, your employer agrees to employ you for a certain number of hours in the year. Annual hours systems are also called annualised hours.

Core hours (n ph). If you work flexible hours, your core hours are the times in the day when you must be at work.

Flexible hours (n ph). See FLEXITIME.

Unsocial hours (n ph). Someone who works unsocial hours does not work at the same time as most other people. For example, if you work through the night, you work unsocial hours.

Working hours (n ph). Your working hours are the number of hours your contract says you should work per day, and the time when you should start and finish work each day.

HOUSE MAGAZINE (n ph)

The house magazine is the magazine written for the employees of a company. It can have several other names including HOUSE JOURNAL, IN-HOUSE MAGAZINE and IN-HOUSE JOURNAL.

> The house magazine can be a very important tool for communicating the company's objectives to its staff.

HUMAN RESOURCES (n phr)

The management of the human resources of a company is the management of all the people used by the company - from inside and outside - to achieve its objectives.

* Human resources development
* Human resources management
* Manage a company's human resources

> Personnel management is the day-to-day management of people; human resources management is the strategic management of people.

JOB (n) jobless (adj, n)

A job is a position of regular paid work in a company. Someone who does not have a job is JOBLESS. See also OCCUPATION, JOB (chapters 3 and 5) and OCCUPATIONAL.

* Get a job
* Lose a job
* A job analysis
* A job code
* Job classification
* A job classification scheme
* Job reclassification
* Job conditions
* Job content
* Job evaluation
* A job evaluation scheme
* A job holder
* Job objectives
* Job rating
* Job satisfaction
* A job seeker
* A job summary
* The jobless rate

> The company plans to create fifty new jobs for skilled and semi-skilled workers.

Job incumbent (n ph). A job incumbent is the person who holds a particular job.

Job security (n ph). If you have job security, you feel fairly sure that you will not lose it.

Job sharing scheme (n ph). A job sharing scheme is a plan which lets two or more people share the same job between them. Job sharers may work split days, split weeks or work alternate weeks. Job sharing can also be called work sharing.

LABOUR (n, v) labourer (n)

Labour is the personnel or the human resources of a company. A LABOURER is an unskilled general worker.

* Labour law
* Labour mobility
* Labour turnover

LEAVE (n)

Leave is holiday or permission to be away from work. This term is often used for expatriates. See also HOLIDAY.

* A leave schedule
* Exceptional leave
* Paid leave
* Post-natal leave
* Relaxation leave
* Sick leave
* Unpaid leave
* Leave entitlement

* Go on leave
* Be on leave
* Grant leave of absence

> I'm afraid you can't talk to Mr Smith because he's away on leave.

Compassionate leave (n ph). If your employer grants you compassionate leave, you have permission to be absent from work for some strong personal reason, for example because a close relative is ill or has died.

Maternity leave (n ph). Maternity leave is the time a woman can take off work to have a baby.

Paternity leave (n ph). Paternity leave is the time a man can take off work to look after a baby or small children.

MANPOWER (n)

The manpower of a company is the total of all the people who work in it. Note: some people think that this word is an example of sexist language and should not be used because it shows prejudice against women. See also PERSONNEL, STAFF, WORKFORCE. These are all neutral terms which can be used instead.

* Manpower demand
* Manpower forecasting
* Manpower forecasting methods
* Manpower planning
* Manpower provision
* Manpower reductions
* Manpower requirements
* Manpower shortage
* Manpower survey

> The personnel department needs to know the company's production targets before it can do any detailed manpower planning.

MANUAL (adj)

Manual workers works with their hands. See also BLUE-COLLAR.

> We think that most of the redundancies will have to be made among the unskilled manual workers in the company.

MORALE (n)

The morale of a company is the general level of satisfaction of the workforce.

* A high level of morale
* A low level of morale

> Morale has been very low since the company announced that there would be job cuts in many departments.

MOTIVATE (v) motivation (n) motive (n)

When you motivate someone, you make them want to work hard and to succeed.

> One of the most important qualities in managers is their ability to motivate their staff.

NOTICE (n)

A notice is a piece of paper with information which is displayed in a place where all employees can read it.

> In many European countries, it is compulsory for companies to display notices about, for example, health and safety and employee representation.

Notice board (n ph). You attach notices to a notice board.

OCCUPATION (n) occupational (adj)

An occupation is a job or a class or category of job. Occupational means job-related. See also JOB.

> The managements of many companies prefer to negotiate with only one union even if it represents members with a number of different occupations.

PART-TIME (adj, adv) part-timer (n)

When you work part-time, you work only part of the standard working week. A part-timer is someone who works part-time. See also HALF-TIME, PART-TIME.

* Part-tiem employment
* Part-time work
* On a part-time basis

> Our policy is to involve our part-time employees in the life of the company as much as the full-time staff.

PERFORM (v) performance (n)

How well you perform in a job is how well you do it.

* Perform a duty, perform duties
* Performance appraisal
* Performance improvement
* Performance management
* A level of performance

> Although he performs his duties satisfactorily, I do not think he is ready for promotion yet.

PERSONNEL (n)

The personnel of the company is the total of all the people who work for it. See also MANPOWER, STAFF, WORKFORCE.

> The personnel of the company were not informed of the new assessment procedures until the last minute.

Personnel management (n ph). Personnel management is concerned with the recruitment, training and development of the workforce of a company.

POSITION (n)

A position is a job. Another word for a position is a POST.

* A key position
* A vacant position
* Fill a vacant position
* Appoint someone to the position of
* Apply for the position of

> The personnel department invites interested staff members to apply for the vacant position of assistant to the marketing director.

SEASONAL (adj)

Seasonal work is work that is available at some times of year but not at others.

* Seasonal employment
* Seasonal job
* Seasonal recruitment
* Seasonal unemployment
* Seasonal work

> A problem for tourist centres is that too many jobs are seasonal so that unemployment goes up when the tourist season ends.

SHIFT (n)

A factory that runs a shift system has one group of workers starting work as soon as another group finishes. Someone on shifts is a SHIFTWORKER.

* A shiftworker
* Shift working
* The day shift
* The night shift
* An eight-hour shift
* Do shift work
* Work shifts

> We have a shift work system to ensure production 24 hours a day throughout the week except on Sunday mornings when the machinery is cleaned and checked.

Three-shift working (n ph). Three-shift working is from, say, 06.00 to 14.00, from 14.00 to 22.00 and from 22.00 to 06.00.

Double-day shift (n ph). The double-day shift is a two shift system, from, say, 06.00 to 14.00 and from 14.00 to 22.00.

Permanent night shift (n ph). A permanent night shift worker always works at night.

> Permanent night shift workers are often paid more for working unsocial hours.

SHOP FLOOR (n ph) or SHOPFLOOR

The shop floor is the place in the factory where goods are produced.

* A shop floor worker

> We hope to improve productivity and increase job satisfaction by encouraging workers on the shop floor to join quality circles where they can talk about their work with their colleagues.

SKILL (n) skilled (adj)

A skill is a special ability or capacity.

* A skills shortage
* A skilled worker
* A semi-skilled worker
* An unskilled worker
* A highly skilled worker
* Acquire skills

> Training and qualifications are very important because new industries often demand high levels of skill from their employees.

STAFF (n,v)

The staff (n) of the company is the total of all the people who work for it. See also MANPOWER, PERSONNEL, WORKFORCE. When you staff (v) a company, you provide it with the work people it needs.

* A member of staff
* A junior member of staff
* A senior member of staff
* A staff shortage
* A serious shortage of staff
* A severe staff shortage
* Contract staff
* Core staff
* Non-core staff

* Secretarial staff
* Technical staff
* Managerial staff
* Supervisory staff
* Staff development
* Staff handbook

> In view of the company's excellent performance this year, all staff have been given one day's extra holiday next month.

SUBORDINATE (n)

Someone who is below you in the organisation is your subordinate.

> Managers should ensure that their subordinates are properly informed about all major developments which affect them.

SUPERIOR (n)

A person who is above you in the hierarchy of an organisation is your superior.

> It is important for the success of a company for all employees to know which superior they should talk to when they have a problem.

Immediate superior (n ph). Your immediate superior is the person directly above you in an organisation.

SUPERVISOR (n) supervise (v) supervisory (adj) supervision (n)

A supervisor is someone in charge of several other (usually blue-collar) workers.

* Supervisory staff
* A supervisory position

> All staff in supervisory positions should carry out their annual assessments before the end of the month.

TEAM (n)

A team is a small group, usually of between four and fifteen people.

* Team building
* Team working
* Build a team
* Work in teams

> Many companies believe that the team is the best basic unit of organisation for their personnel.

TELEWORK (n) teleworker (n) teleworking (n)

Telework is work for a company which you do at home. Teleworkers can spend some or all of their time working at home. they often have telephones, faxes and computers for communication with their company. Teleworking is also called TELECOMMUTING. Teleworkers are also called HOMEWORKERS.

> Teleworking can help companies save money because they spend less on office space, lighting and heating, canteen facilities and so on.

TERMS (n pl)

The terms of an agreement or contract are the conditions which an employer and an employee agree to.

* Agree on terms
* The terms of an agreement
* The terms of the contract
* Under the terms of the contract
* Terms of employment

> Under the terms of the new agreement, staff will work an extra half hour two afternoons per week in exchange for a half day off every fourth Friday in the month.

TIME OFF (n ph)

If you take time off work, you do not do your usual work for a period which could vary from just a few minutes up to several months. Taking time off can be both paid and unpaid.

* Take time off work to

> He's taken some time off this afternoon to go to the hospital for a checkup.

TURNOVER (n)

The turnover in personnel of a company is the number of people being replaced each year expressed as a percentage of the whole workforce: if a company has 200 employees and turnover is 10% for the year, it means that 20 of the staff have left and have been replaced by new employees.

* Labour turnover
* High staff turnover
* Low staff turnover

> High staff turnover can affect both the quality of a company's products and the morale of its workforce.

VACATION (n,v)

A vacation is a period of time when you do not have to go to work. See also HOLIDAY.

* Take a vacation
* Go on vacation

> He's between jobs so he's taking a long vacation.

WHITE-COLLAR (adj phr)

A white-collar worker works in an office. See also BLUE-COLLAR.
> Union membership is increasing among our white-collar staff but decreasing among the blue-collar workers.

WORK (n,v) worker (n) working (adj)

* Workplace
* Work environment
* Working arrangements
* Flexible working arrangements
* Working conditions
* Working days
* Working hours
* Working practice
* Good working practice
* Flexible working
* Work for

> The staff said that they wanted a big improvement in their working conditions, including longer breaks, a better canteen and tighter safety regulations.
> The working day of our white collar staff is from 09.00 to 05.00 with a one-hour break for lunch.

Off work (adv ph).If you are off work, you are absent from work, for example because you are sick.

Work sharing (n ph). See JOB; Job sharing scheme.

Working group (n ph). A working group is a temporary committee created to discuss and recommend how to solve a particular problem.

Autonomous working group (n ph). An autonomous working group is a team of workers, usually working in factory production, which can make more decisions than usual about the best way to work without asking a superior.

Peripheral worker (n ph). A peripheral worker is an employee who does not work full-time.

WORKFORCE (n)

The workforce of a company is the total of all the people who work for it. See also MANPOWER, PERSONNEL, STAFF.

> The whole of our workforce is now involved in improving our products and services.

Single status workforce (n ph). A single status workforce is one which treats white-collar and blue-collar workers in the same way.

Chapter 2

Philosophy, Policy and Planning

How many of these terms can you use?

AFFIRMATIVE ACTION   BENCHMARK   CASUAL WORK
    CODE OF PRACTICE   COWBOY OPERATOR   DELAYER
DEMANNING   DEMOTE   DIRECTIVE
DISABILITY   DISCHARGE   DISCRIMINATE
    DISMISS   DOWNSIZE   EMPOWER
EQUAL OPPORTUNITIES   EXIT INTERVIEW   EXPATRIATE
    FEATHERBEDDING   FIRE   FREELANCER
FREE MOVEMENT OF LABOUR   GLASS CEILING   GOAL
    HIRE AND FIRE   LAST IN, FIRST OUT   LAY OFF
    MAN   NATURAL WASTAGE   NOTICE
    OUTPLACEMENT   OUTSOURCE   OVERMAN
OVERSTAFF   POSITION ANALYSIS   QUESTIONNAIRE
    POSITIVE ACTION   POST   PREDECESSOR
PRE-RETIREMENT   PROMOTE   QUIT
    QUOTA STRATEGY   RATE   REDEPLOY
    REDUNDANCT   RELEASE   RELOCATE
REMOVAL   RESETTLE   RESIGN
    RETAIN STAFF   RETIRE   RETURNER
    ROSTER   SABBATICAL   SACK
SECOND   SENIORITY   SHELTERED
    SHORT-TIME WORKING   SIDEWAYS MOVE
STAGGER   STAKEHOLDER   SUCCEED
SUGGESTION   SURVIVOR   TERMINATION
THIRD COUNTRY NATIONAL   TIME AND MOTION STUDY
    TRANSFER OF UNDERTAKINGS

Exercise 1

Complete the following sentences by deciding which of the choices A, B, C or D fits best.

1. We employ large numbers of . . . .
   in the summer when production is twice as high as usual.

   A. occasional people   B. returned employees   C. casual workers
   D. freelancers

2. The company will . . . . him soon so he should get more
   money and a bigger office.

   A. demote   B. promote   C. dismiss   D. retire

3. His work was so unsatisfactory that finally we had to . . . .
   him.

   A. dismiss   B. return   C. recruit   D. resign

4. The economic situation has been so bad recently that local companies
   have had to . . . . several thousand workers.

   A. lay up   B. lay off   C. lay down   D. lay by

5. It is important for organisations to define their . . . . and
   it is also very important that everyone in the organisation knows what
   they are.

   A. objects   B. scores   C. penalties   D. goals

6. It is in my contract of employment that if I want to leave the company I have to give three months' . . . .

    A. note   B. delay   C. notice   D. statement

7. That company is so . . . . that some employees have absolutely nothing to do.

    A. overstaffed   B. understaffed   C. overworked   D. overpowered

8. To cut costs and to improve the lifestyles of our employees, we have decided to . . . . from the city to a small country town.

    A. remove   B. return   C. relocate   D. resettle

Exercise 2

Complete the following text with the appropriate word or phrase selected from the box below.

Redundant	Downsizing	Retirement	Goal
Outplacement counselling		Natural wastage	Early retirement

. . . . the workforce is a major part of this company's rationalisation programme. Our . . . . is a 10% reduction in the workforce in the next two years. We think that most of this reduction can be achieved through . . . . : a number of our older staff are coming up to . . . . age and others may be interested in taking .
. . . . We hope that only a few people

will actually be made . . . . All these people will be given
extensive . . . .

Exercise 3

Complete the spaces in the following text by adding appropriate words or
phrases.

Two years ago, when we became an e . . . . o . . . .
employer, we took a long hard look at the way women were treated in the
company and decided that we needed to make a lot of changes. Not enough
women were getting p . . . . to the top jobs: there was a
g . . . . c . . . . stopping women from being
appointed to the most senior positions. So we decided to take a . . . .
a . . . . to improve the situation. We recruited more women.
Our p . . . . a . . . . training programme
helped women to improve their skills. We even changed the language we used
and started to talk about overstaffing rather than o . . . . We
still have a long way to go but we have definitely made progress.

AFFIRMATIVE ACTION (n ph)

A company which takes affirmative action makes extra efforts to recruit women and members of ethnic minorities as a way of reducing discrimination against these groups. See also POSITIVE ACTION, QUOTA STRATEGY.

* An affirmative action programme
* Take affirmative action

> Companies, in the US in particular, introduce affirmative action programmes as a way of improving the position of women and of minorities.

BENCHMARK (n, v) benchmarking (n)

When a company benchmarks some part of its operation, it looks in detail at what other successful competitors do, defines a best practice, and then uses the information to improve its own performance in this area.

> Benchmarking is a "You-show-me-yours-and-I'll-show-you-mine" way of getting ahead of competitors by measuring your own performance against theirs.

CASUAL WORK (n phr) casual worker (n phr)

Casual work is work done for a short period. A casual worker is someone who works for an employer from time to time, not full-time. Casual work is also called CASUAL LABOUR.

> Companies use casual labour to increase production when there is a sudden increase in demand.

Casualisation (n). We talk about the casualisation of the workforce when more and more of the employees of a company are part-time or temporary workers.

CODE OF PRACTICE (n ph)

A code of practice, for example a code of practice for disabled people or for health and safety, is a written set of rules for a certain area of work.

 * We think the government's new code of practice on health and safety administration is good but we are worried about how much it will cost us to implement.

COWBOY OPERATOR (n ph)

A cowboy operator is an agency, consultant or company which provides bad service.

> Although some people think that many consultants are cowboy operators, research shows that many of them work very hard at relatively little profit.

DELAYER (v)

When a company delayers, it flattens the structure of the organisation in order to create more flexibility and more self management.

> When companies delayer, there is a danger that although job satisfaction and individual responsibility increases, job insecurity also increases and promotion opportunities get worse.

DEMANNING (n)

When there is demanning in a company, people lose their jobs. Note: some people think that this word is an example of sexist language and should not be used because it shows prejudice against women. See also MAN, OVERMAN, REDUNDANT.

> There has been a lot of demanning among local companies recently due to the economic downturn.

DEMOTE (v) demotion (n)

When you demote someone, you give them a lower grade job. DEMOTE is the opposite of PROMOTE.

* Suffer a demotion

> Everybody thinks that his recent change of job is really a demotion although he says that it is a change of responsibilities.

DIRECTIVE (n)

A directive recommends a country, an organisation or a business to act in a particular way.

* An EU directive
* Issue a directive

> The EU has issued directives on a wide range of personnel subjects including health and safety, wage payment systems and training.

DISABILITY (n) disable (v) disabled (adj)

Someone with a disability has some kind of physical or mental injury, handicap or illness. See also SHELTERED.

* Partially disabled
* Severely disabled
* Disabled employment
* Disability benefit
* A disability pension
* A disability plan
* A disability scheme

> A good disability insurance plan ought to cover employees for most, if not all, kinds of disability resulting from industrial accidents.

DISCHARGE (n,v)

If an employer discharges you, you lose your job and must leave the company. See also DISMISS, FIRE, SACK.

> Normally a company must give notice of its intention to discharge large numbers of members of the workforce.

DISCRIMINATE (v) discrimination (n) discriminatory (adj)

If you discriminate against a person, you treat that person unfairly.

* Discriminate against
* An act of discrimination
* Age discrimination
* Racial discrimination
* Sex discrimination / Sexual discrimination
* Unlawful discrimination
* Discrimination on the grounds of race, creed or colour
* A discriminatory practice

> The British Sex Discrimination Act of 1975 encourages the equal treatment of men and women in employment and in other areas.

DISMISS (v) dismissal (n)

If an employer dismisses an employee, the employee no longer has a job and must leave the company. See also DISCHARGE, FIRE, SACK, TERMINATION.

* Liable to dismissal
* Instant dismissal

> Workers found smoking cigarettes in this part of the factory are liable to instant dismissal.

Fair dismissal (n ph). In a case of fair dismissal, an employee is dismissed with good reason.

Unfair dismissal (n ph). In a case of unfair dismissal, an employee is dismissed without good reason.

* A claim of unfair dismissal

Wrongful dismissal (n ph). In a case of wrongful dismissal, an employee is dismissed in a way which is not legally correct.

* A claim of wrongful dismissal

> Employees who think they have been unfairly or wrongfully dismissed, can take the case to an industrial relations tribunal.

DOWNSIZE (v)

When a company downsizes, it makes itself smaller by cutting staff.

> He was made redundant as a result of a major downsizing operation at his company.

EMPOWER (v) empowerment (n)

Empowered employees can make important decisions about how they do their work without having to ask a superior. Empowered employees believe that they share responsibility for the success of their company.

* An empowered organisation

> Our empowerment campaign has helped our staff members understand that they are all important and that they can all help the company to do better.

EQUAL OPPORTUNITIES (n ph)

The objective of an equal opportunities policy is to ensure that a company's male and female employees are treated equally.

* An equal opportunities policy
* Committed to an equal opportunities policy

> Equal opportunities policies should pay special attention, among other things, to selection and training procedures, promotion, pay and hours.

Equal opportunities employer (n ph). Equal opportunities employers aim to remove discrimination on the grounds of sex, race, religion, marital status, disability and age.

EXIT INTERVIEW (n ph)

You may have an exit interview with a manager before you leave a company. See also TERMINATION, INTERVIEW.

> Some companies hold exit interviews with all departing personnel to find out why they are leaving.

EXPATRIATE (adj, n) expatriation (n)

Expatriates work abroad for their companies. See also THIRD COUNTRY NATIONAL.

> Some human resources divisions have sections which work only on expatriate questions.

FEATHERBEDDING (n) featherbed (v)

Featherbedding is employing more staff than a company really needs. See also OVERMAN, OVERSTAFF.

> The company's aim in negotiating a single union agreement is to reduce the amount of featherbedding which has traditionally taken place.

FIRE (v)

If your employer fires you, he tells you that you no longer have a job and that you must leave the company. FIRE is an informal word. See also DISCHARGE, DISMISS, HIRE AND FIRE, SACK and TERMINATION.

> He was fired for stealing.

FREELANCER (n) freelance (adj, v)

Freelancers are self-employed, usually professional people, who may work for one company for a limited period, for example as a consultant, but who normally have a range of clients. See also OUTSOURCE.

* Work freelance
* Go freelance, decide to go freelance

> It was a big decision for me to go freelance but, with so many companies outsourcing work, it has proved to be a profitable one.

FREE MOVEMENT OF LABOUR (n ph)

When there is free movement of labour between two or more countries, workers of one nationality can get work in another country in the same way as in their own country.

> Although there is free movement of labour between member states of the European Union in principle, there are still many rules in the different countries which stop this happening in practice.

GLASS CEILING (n ph)

The glass ceiling is the invisible barrier which prevents more women from getting promotion to top company positions.

> Although the proportion of women in some professions is increasing, there must still be a glass ceiling in business since so few women are at the head of major companies.

GOAL (n)

A goal is an objective or a target.

* Attain a goal
* Meet a goal
* Reach a goal
* Set a goal

> We set goals for all our employees and we make bonus payments to people who reach their goals.

Goal setting (n ph). Goal setting means fixing objectives.

HIRE AND FIRE (v ph, adj ph)

When a company hires and fires people, it recruits and dismisses staff frequently. See also HIRE.

* A hire and fire approach

> Companies which hire and fire do not normally show much sense of responsibility for their employees.

> The employees of companies which hire and fire do not usually feel a strong sense of loyalty to their employers.

LAST IN, FIRST OUT (adj ph)

A company with a last in, first out policy chooses for redundancy first the person that it recruited the most recently. Last in, first out is sometimes referred to as LIFO.

* Operate a last in, first out policy

> Because of the current economic difficulties facing the firm, and since we operate a last in, first out policy, we regret to inform you that we plan to make redundant all employees recruited since the beginning of the year.

LAY OFF (v, n)

When a company lays off staff, it dismisses them temporarily because there is not enough work for them to do.

> We have to lay off a certain number of workers due to a fall in sales but we hope to take them all on again as soon as the economic situation improves.

MAN (v) manning (n)

When you man a task, you provide the people for the job to be completed. Note: some people think that this word is an example of sexist language and should not be used because it shows prejudice against women. See also DEMANNING, OVERMAN.

* A manning agreement
* A manning level

> Because of automation, manning levels are lower than they have ever been in many manufacturing industries.

NATURAL WASTAGE (n ph)

When a company's workforce gets smaller through natural wastage, it is because employees retire, die or leave the company and are not replaced.

> We do not want to make anyone redundant so we hope we can reduce the size of the workforce by 20% over the next five years through natural wastage alone.

NOTICE (n)

A period of notice is the length of time that you have to work between the date when you resign from or are dismissed from your job and the date when you actually leave the company. See also NOTICE (chapter 1).

* Hand in one's notice
* Give notice
* Give one's notice

* Notice to quit
* Receive notice
* Three months' notice

> All our employees must give a minimum of one month's notice of their intention to leave the company.

OUTPLACEMENT (n)

Outplacement means redundancy. During outplacement, the employer usually gives employees help in preparing themselves to find another job. Another term for outplacement is RESETTLEMENT. See also TERMINATION.

* Outplacement counselling

> We provide outplacement support in the form of counselling, advice about how to write a CV and retraining programmes for all staff made redundant.

OUTSOURCE (v) outsourcing (n)

When a company outsources a service, it decides to stop employing people directly to provide the service and asks an outside agency to provide it instead. Outsourcing is also known as OUTSERVICING.

> We decided to outsource our cleaning and canteen facilities to outside suppliers in order to cut costs.

OVERMAN (v) overmanning (n)

An overmanned company has too many staff. Note: some people think that this word is an example of sexist language and should not be used because it shows prejudice against women. See also DEMAN, FEATHERBEDDING, MAN, OVERSTAFF.

> We need a leaner organisation and that means reducing overmanning which obviously exists in some departments.

OVERSTAFF (v) overstaffing (n)

When a company is overstaffed, it has too many people working for it. See also FEATHERBEDDING, OVERMAN.

* Suffer from overstaffing

> The only way we can solve our problems of overstaffing is by making unproductive staff redundant.

POSITION ANALYSIS QUESTIONNAIRE (n ph)

A position analysis questionnaire is a detailed questionnaire used by a job analyst to describe a job. A position analysis questionnaire is also known as JOB ANALYSIS QUESTIONNAIRE.

* Fill in a position analysis questionnaire
* Complete a position analysis questionnaire

> Some personnel managers find the quantitative approach of the PAQ very useful in deciding on the pay for a particular job.

POSITIVE ACTION (n ph)

When employers take positive action, they create opportunities, for example, through training, for members of one sex to do a job which before had been done only by members of the other sex. See also AFFIRMATIVE ACTION.

* Take positive action

> In spite of our positive action programme, we still have no male secretaries, no male cleaners and no female directors.

POST (v) posting (n)

When your company posts you somewhere, it sends you somewhere else to work for a period, usually abroad. A posting lasts at least several months, and is usually for at least a year. See also POSITION.

* A foreign posting
* A posting abroad
* Send someone on a posting abroad

> Senior executives in multinationals should gain international experience in several foreign postings during their careers.

PREDECESSOR (n)

Your predecessor is the person who held your current position before you.

> It took me a long time to do this job well because my predecessor was so disorganised.

PRE-RETIREMENT (n)

Pre-retirement is the period in your working life before you retire when you begin to prepare for retirement. See also RETIRE.

> The company offers pre-retirement counselling not only to employees retiring soon but also to their spouses.

PROMOTE (v) promotion (n)

When you promote someone, you give them a higher grade job. The opposite of PROMOTE is DEMOTE.

* Good promotion prospects
* Poor promotion prospects

* Promotion opportunities
* Promotion by seniority

> He was promoted to the post of Head of Department at the age of 39, the youngest we have ever had.

QUIT (v)

When you quit your job, you leave the company you were working for. See also NOTICE, RESIGN.

> The best thing I ever did was to quit my old job and start my own company.

QUOTA STRATEGY (n ph)

A company with a quota strategy has a rule that some vacancies can only be filled, for example, by women or disabled or black people. See AFFIRMATIVE ACTION, POSITIVE ACTION.

> Some people think that a quota strategy is a good way to help members of minorities to advance but others think that it can create a situation where vacancies do not always go to the best applicants.

RATE (n, v) rating (n)

When you rate something, you measure how good it is. See also RATE (chapter 4), RATING DRIFT.

* give a rating to
* a rating scale
* the going rate

> All the employees in the company were asked to rate their job satisfaction using a rating scale of 1 - 10.

REDEPLOY (v) redeployment (n) redeployee (n)

If your company redeploys you, it transfers you to another job when your old one is cut.

> For companies facing cutbacks, redeployment is a more caring alternative than redundancy but is complicated to manage.

REDUNDANT (adj) redundancy (n)

If you are made redundant, you lose your job. See also TERMINATION.

* Make someone redundant
* A compulsory redundancy
* A voluntary redundancy
* A redundancy notice
* Serve a redundancy notice on
* Redundancy counselling
* Redundancy terms

* Generous redundancy terms
* Serve a redundancy notice on

> We have to reduce the workforce and so we have served redundancy notices on 100 employees, informing them that their jobs will be cut as from 1 January.

Redundancy package (n ph). You get a redundancy package from your employer when you lose your job and receive both money and training to help you find another job.
Redundancy packages are also known as severance packages.

RELEASE (v, n)

When a company releases an employee, it makes the employee redundant. "Release" is a euphemism. See also RELEASE (chapter 5), TERMINATION.

> Due to the recent restructuring of the company, we have had to release 500 of our workforce.

RELOCATE (v) relocation (n)

When a company relocates, it moves from one place to another. See REMOVAL.

* A relocation allowance
* Relocation expenses

> Employees are often against relocation when they are first told that their company wants them to move from a city to a smaller town, but many of them are eventually very happy about the change.

REMOVAL (n) remove(v)

A removals service is one which moves your furniture and other belongings from your old home to your new one. See RELOCATE.

> When the company relocated from the capital to the provinces, it paid the removals expenses of all its personnel.

RESETTLE (v) resettlement (n)

When a company resettles you, it helps you to move back to the place where you used to live and work before you moved to live and work in another place.

* A resettlement allowance

> Managers returning to their own country from a job abroad should not have too much problem settling down again if they have a generous resettlement allowance.

RESIGN (v) resignation (n)

When you resign, you tell your employer that you want to give up your current job and (usually) to leave the company. See also NOTICE, QUIT, TERMINATION.

* accept someone's resignation
* hand in your resignation
* offer your resignation

> After a third year of poor figures, the Managing Director offered his resignation to the Board. The Board accepted it.

RETAIN STAFF (v ph) retention of staff (n ph)

A company which tries to retain staff makes efforts to keep its employees and to encourage them not to leave.

> As the shortage of skilled workers in the West grows, more and more companies try to retain the staff that they already have.

RETIRE (v) retirement (n)

When you retire, you give up your job because you have reached the age - often 60 or 65 years old - when the government or the company says you must stop working. See also PRE-RETIREMENT, TERMINATION.

* Early retirement
* Take early retirement
* Reach retirement age

> In our company, men and women retire at 65.
> One way for a company to reduce the size of its workforce is to encourage its older members of staff to take early retirement.

RETURNER (n)

A returner is a woman who rejoins a company after having spent some years away from work, raising a family.

> Companies are now trying hard to recruit returners because of their maturity and experience.

ROSTER (n)

A roster is a list of employees and their duties or the times when they are on duty.

* A duty roster

> The oil rig supervisor posts the duty roster for the coming week on the main noticeboard outside the canteen every Thursday afternoon.

SABBATICAL (n)

When you take a sabbatical, your company gives you permission to take a few months off from your normal job so that you can undertake a special project, for example to do research or to write a book.

* On sabbatical
* Grant a sabbatical
* Take a sabbatical
* Take sabbatical leave

> His company has granted him a sabbatical term which he plans to spend at the local university doing research.

SACK (v)

If your employer sacks you, he tells you that you no longer have a job and that you must leave the company. SACK is an informal word. See also DISCHARGE, DISMISS, FIRE and HIRE, TERMINATION.

* A sackable offence

> The supervisor warned him that smoking in the production area was a sackable offence and that if he didn't put out his cigarette straightaway, he would probably lose his job.

SECOND (v) secondment (n)

When a company seconds employees, it transfers them temporarily to another part of the company or lends them to another organisation for a certain period of time.

* on secondment

> Although she normally works in the personnel department of a large company, she is currently on secondment to a charity dealing with homeless people.

SENIORITY (n)

A company which operates a seniority rule promotes people according to how long they have worked for the company rather than according to merit.

* Operate a / the seniority rule

> The company always used to appoint managers to the top posts by seniority but now it is done much more according to merit and ability.

SHELTERED (adj)

A sheltered situation is one specially designed for a disabled person. For example, a sheltered factory is one where a majority of the employees are disabled. See also DISABILITY.

* A sheltered job
* A sheltered placement scheme

> According to research in Britain, many disabled people prefer to work in sheltered jobs in sheltered factories rather than in "open" employment.

SHORT-TIME WORKING (n ph)

When a company puts some of its employees on short-time working, it employs them for fewer hours than usual each week because it does not have enough work for them to do.

* Put someone on short-time working
* Restore someone to full-time working

> We hope to restore all employees from short-time to full-time working as soon as the economic situation permits.

SIDEWAYS MOVE (n ph)

A job change which is neither a promotion nor a demotion is called a sideways move.

* Make a sideways move

> He expected to be promoted during the reorganisation but in fact his new job is only a sideways move.

STAGGER (v)

When a company staggers the holidays of its employees, it organises them so that not everyone goes on holiday at the same time, in order to be sure that the work of the company goes on smoothly.

* Staggered holidays
* Staggered hours

> The summer holidays of our workforce are staggered from June to September so that not too many people are away at any one time.

STAKEHOLDER (n)

A stakeholder is anyone who has some interest in encouraging the success of a company. Stakeholders can include the shareholders of the company, its employees and their families, and its customers.

> More and more companies say they feel a responsibility to all of their stakeholders and not just their shareholders.

SUCCEED (v) succession (n) successor (n)

You succeed someone when you take a job from another person. You are that person's successor. See also PREDECESSOR.

> Since I shall be retiring very shortly, I have passed on your letter to my successor, Ms Smith, who will deal with your request.

Succession planning (n ph). Succession planning is planning who will take over which job from whom and when.

SUGGESTION (n) suggest (v)

When you make a suggestion, you propose to the company a way of doing something better.

* A suggestion scheme
* Run a suggestion scheme

> A good suggestions scheme can lead to reduced costs, improved profitability and improved communication. Some companies give prizes for suggestions which save them money.

Suggestions box (n ph). A suggestions box is a box into which employees can put paper on which they have written ideas for doing things better within the company.

SURVIVOR (n)

Survivors are the employees who are left after a company has made a lot of others redundant.

> Counselling can help survivors to overcome typical feelings of decreased motivation and morale and increased levels of stress after a company has made large-scale redundancies.

TERMINATION (n) terminate (v)

Termination is a general word for the different ways of ending a job, through retirement, resignation, redundancy, and so on. See also DISMISS, EXIT INTERVIEW, FIRE, OUTPLACEMENT, REDUNDANT, RELEASE, RESIGN, RETIRE, SACK.

* A termination interview
* A termination report
* Notification of termination
* Settlement on termination of employment

THIRD COUNTRY NATIONAL (n ph)

A third country national is someone with a passport from one country who is employed in another country by a company from a third country. A third country national is often known as a TCN.

> We have had to ask a specialist insurance company to help us calculate the insurance needs and pension rights of the many third country nationals who we employ around the world.

TIME AND MOTION STUDY (n ph)

Time and motion is a technique for studying how to increase the output from a job by measuring and analysing in detail how the job is done and how long each part of the job takes to do.

* A time and motion study

> Time and motion studies carried out by consultants have been very unpopular with workers in the past but more recent experiments with workers doing the measuring themselves have been much more successful.

TRANSFER OF UNDERTAKINGS (n ph)

There is a transfer of undertakings when one organisation passes responsibility for an activity to another.

> European Union rules give employees some protection of their pay and working conditions under the new employer when a transfer of undertakings takes place.

Chapter 3

Recruitment and Selection

How many of these terms can you use?

CANDIDATE ADVERTISE APPLICANT

TESTIMONIAL APPLICATION PROBATIONARY PERIOD

APPOINTMENT PROFILE WORD OF MOUTH

SEARCH CV EXECUTIVE SEARCH AGENCY

HEAD HUNT REQUIREMENTS

REFERENCE GRAPHOLOGY INTERVIEWER SCREEN

RECRUIT SELECTION TEST

TRACK RECORD MEDICAL EXAMINATION EXPERIENCE

MILK ROUND APPOINT PANEL

PRE-SELECT APPLY QUALIFICATION

INTAKE REFEREE GRADUATE

RÉSUMÉ INTERVIEW

SALARY SELECT SHORTLIST

TAKE ON RECRUITMENT VACANT

REJECT VACANCY

Exercise 1

Complete the following sentences by deciding which of the choices A, B, C or D fits best.

1. Her CV was so interesting that we called her to ask if she could come for an . . . . the following day.

    A. appointment   B. interview   C. attendance   D. opportunity

2. We had so many applications that we have had to . . . . some very interesting ones.

    A. reject   B. sack   C. outplace   D. retire

3. Staff members are invited to . . . . for the post of Deputy Quality Assurance Manager.

    A. recruit   B. position   C. appoint   D. apply

4. We wish to . . . . someone to replace the Director of Production before the end of the month.

    A. appoint   B. experience   C. referee   D. qualify

5. We have plans to . . . . ten more people to the Production division before the end of the month.

    A. recruit   B. take up   C. obtain   D. have

6. There has been a . . . . position in the Personnel Department since before Christmas but we can't find anyone to fill it.

    A. empty   B. vacant   C. unfulfilled   D. unemployed

7. We gave him the job because he was obviously the best . . . .

    A. claimant   B. graduate   C. recruit   D. candidate.

8. It was difficult to . . . . from among so many strong people but
    finally we chose the one with the most experience.

    A. single   B. prefer   C. select   D. sort

Exercise 2

CV	shortlist	track record	graduates
qualifications	confidential	medical examination	advertise

Complete each of the following sentences with one of the words or phrases in
the box.

1. After reading all the letters of application, we drew up a . . . .
    of six applicants.

2. I should be grateful if you would treat my application as . . . .
    until I have had a chance to explain my position to my current employer.

3. Since we did not succeed in recruiting anyone locally, we decided to
    . . . . in the national press.

4. When writing a . . . . it is important to give your full
    name, address, telephone number and date of birth as well as details of
    your education, qualifications and experience.

5.	Since this job is open only to . . . . , there's no point in applying if you don't have a university degree.

6.	His previous career looked very impressive, but since he joined this company, his . . . . has been very disappointing.

7.	In France, all employees must have an annual . . . . to check that they are in good health.

8.	The . . . . for this job include a university degree, an ability to speak two foreign languages and at least three years' previous experience.

Exercise 3

Complete the following text with appropriate words or phrases.

When a company decides to fill a v . . . . position, the first thing it may do is to a . . . . the post internally. It will invite a . . . . from all q . . . . personnel: in some companies the applicants will have to c . . . . a form, while in others they will have to write a letter and send this together with a c . . . . v . . . . to the person in charge of r . . . .

Sometimes there are not enough good internal c . . . . and then the company may a . . . . .in the national or specialised press. Once a good number of a . . . . have been received, the company draws up a s . . . . of two or three. These are invited to the company for i . . . .

This stage may last a few minutes or several days. The a . . . . may have to answer questions from one person or from a p . . . . of several i . . . . They may learn the result of the i . . . . straight away or only after several days or even weeks. The company may want time to ask for r . . . .

Finally the company will make the decision to accept one c . . . . and to r . . . . the others. Of course it is important for the company to make the right decision: mistakes can be costly!

ADVERTISE (v) advertisement (n) ad (n)

When you advertise a job vacancy, you pay for information about the job to appear in newspapers or specialised magazines.

* A job advertisement
* Place an advertisement
* Advertise a vacancy
* Advertise in the national press
* Advertise nationally
* Advertise in the specialised press

> Big companies normally advertise important vacancies both in the national and in the specialised press.

APPLY (v) applicant (n) application (n)

When you apply for a job, you tell the company formally that you would like the job. Someone who applies for a job is an APPLICANT.

* Apply for a job
* Apply for the post of
* A job applicant
* A letter of application
* A written application
* An application form
* An application procedure
* Fill in an application form
* Complete an application form
* Make an application for the post of
* Submit an application
* Send a completed application form to
* Invite applications from
* Reject an application
* The status of an application

> Companies should always reply to all the letters of application they receive.

Spontaneous application (n ph). When you make a spontaneous application, you write to a company asking for a job even though they have not advertised a vacancy.

Consider an application (v ph). A company considering an application is thinking about it and has not yet made a decision.

Turn down an application (v ph). When a company turns down your application, it tells you that it is not going to give you a job.

APPOINT (v) appointee (n) appointment (n)

When a company appoints someone to a post, it formally gives the job to that person. Someone who is appointed to a post is an APPOINTEE.

* Make an appointment
* A first appointment

> Senior company appointments are announced in the business appointments sections of the national newspapers.

CANDIDATE (n) candidature (n)

When you apply for a job, you become a candidate for the job.

* A successful candidate
* An unsuccessful candidate
* A strong candidate
* A weak candidate

> When there are a lot of applicants for a post, the recruiter has to draw up a shortlist of no more than six candidates.

CV (abbrev)

Your CV is a formal document giving details of your education and professional history which you send to a company when you apply for a job. CV stands for CURRICULUM VITAE (Latin).

* Send a copy of one's CV

> Send your CV together with a letter of application, a recent photograph, and the names and addresses of two referees.

EXECUTIVE SEARCH AGENCY (n phr)

An executive search agency is a consultancy which helps companies to recruit (usually) senior managers. Executive search consultants are also known as head hunters. See also: HEAD HUNTER, SEARCH.

* Carry out an executive search
* An executive search consultant

> Companies often complain that executive search agencies are expensive but they sometimes have to use them, for example when they are trying to recruit managers in another country where they have no local staff.

EXPERIENCE (n)

The experience you have is the knowledge and skill you have obtained from your current and your previous jobs.

* Wide experience
* Limited experience
* Job experience
* Professional experience

* Previous experience
* A wealth of experience

> We are looking for someone with wide experience of accounting systems in several European countries.

GRADUATE (n,v)

A graduate is someone with a university degree.

* Graduate recruitment
* A graduate recruit
* A postgraduate
* A postgraduate degree

> The recruitment officers of many big British companies travel round the universities once a year in order to meet future graduates who could be potential recruits.

GRAPHOLOGY (n) graphologist (n)

Graphology is the study of handwriting in order to learn about the personality of the writer. Graphology tests are also known as HANDWRITING TESTS.

> It is quite common in France for employers to ask graphologists to analyse examples of job candidates' handwriting.

HEAD HUNT (v ph) head hunter (n ph)

When an executive search agency head hunts a manager, it persuades him or her to leave his or her current job in order to work for another company which is paying the agency to fill the vacancy. See also: EXECUTIVE SEARCH AGENCY, SEARCH.

> In France, head hunters can begin their searches by using data bases of names of graduates of the top business and engineering schools.

INTAKE (n)

An intake is a group of people all recruited at the same time.

* An annual intake
> Because of the economic situation, our annual intake of high fliers is smaller than usual but contains some very good people.

INTERVIEW (n,v) interviewee (n) interviewer (n)

An interview is a meeting between a job applicant and someone in the company who will decide or help to decide whether to give a job to this person.

* Call a candidate to interview
* Hold an interview
* Invite the candidate to attend an interview

* Performance in the interview, interview performance
* The final interview
* Reach the final interview stage
* A group interview
* An informal interview
* A preliminary interview

> Although he was invited to attend a preliminary interview for the vacant post, he did not reach the final interview stage.

Attend an interview (v ph). When a candidate attends an interview, he or she is present at the interview.

Hold an interview (v ph). When companies hold interviews, they organise interviews to which they invite shortlisted applicants.

JOB (n)

A job is a position of regular paid work in a company. See also JOB (chapter 1).

* A job advertisement
* A job application
* A job application form
* A job description
* A job interview
* A job interview
* A job offer
* A job specification
* A job vacancy
* Apply for a job
* Offer a job to

> Job applicants are normally sent a job description or job specification and a job application form.

Job prospects (n ph). If you have a good chance of future promotion, your job prospects are good.

MEDICAL EXAMINATION (n phr)

When you have a medical examination, a doctor or nurse checks that your physical and mental condition is good enough for the job you have applied for.

> A medical examination is often a compulsory part of the job application process.

MILK ROUND (n ph)

The Milk Round in Britain is the unofficial name for the annual tour of British universities made by the recruitment officers of major companies in search of talented future graduates.

> The number of vacancies being advertised each year by companies doing the Milk Round is one indicator of the state of the British economy.

PANEL (n)

A panel is a small group of interviewers.

* An interview panel
* A selection panel

> Some selection procedures involve several stages including interviews with a single interviewer and panel interviews.

PRE-SELECT (v) pre-selection (n)

When you receive a lot of applications for a post, you may do a pre-selection of a certain number of applicants as a first step in the recruitment process. See also SELECT, SHORTLIST.

> When the company received more than 2,000 applications for six vacancies, it pre-selected 400 to go on to the next stage.

PROBATIONARY PERIOD (n ph)

A probationary period is a trial period of a few weeks or months after you start a new job during which you or your employer can still decide not to make the appointment permanent.

* Extension of probationary period

> His work was so bad that the company would not keep him on after the end of his three-month probationary period.

PROFILE (n, v)

A profile is a short written summary giving the main features of something.

* Individual profile
* Job profile
* Career profile

> Companies get information about job applicants from their CVs, from a completed application form, or from a letter written by the candidate which contains an individual profile of his or her previous job experience.

QUALIFICATION (n)

A qualification is an official recognition that you have successfully completed a course of education or training.

* Formal qualifications
* No formal qualifications
* An academic qualification
* A professional qualification
* A recognized qualification

* Well qualified
* Poorly qualified

> For many managerial jobs, you need either an academic qualification like a degree or a professional qualification from a professional body or both.

Practical qualifications (n ph). If you have good practical qualifications, you have a lot of experience in a particular area, even if you do not have any formal qualifications for the job.

RECRUIT (v, n) recruitment (n)

When a company recruits someone, it finds and employs someone to do a particular job.

* A graduate recruit
* A recruitment agency
* A recruitment procedure
* The recruitment process
* Stages in the recruitment process
* External recruitment
* Internal recruitment
* Graduate recruitment

> The recruitment process can range from a few minutes of basic questions to several weeks of different stages of interviews and tests.

Recruitment drive (n ph). When a company needs to recruit quite a lot of people at the same time, it organises a recruitment drive.

* Mount a recruitment drive

Recruitment officer (n ph). The job of a company recruitment officer is to find new employees for the company.

REFEREE (n), reference (n)

A referee is a person who agrees to tell a company about a job applicant's professional or personal abilities and capacities. The company then contacts your referees to ask for a REFERENCE.

* Approach a referee
* Act as a referee
* Agree to act as a referee
* Ask for a reference, ask for references
* Ask the candidate's permission to follow up references
* Follow up references
* Grant permission to follow up references
* Provide a reference
* Provide a written reference
* A personal reference
* A character reference
* A professional reference

> If a company is interested in your application, it will follow up your references by approaching your referees before your interview.

REJECT (v) rejection (n)

A company rejects an application when it tells the applicant that it does not want to give him or her the job.

> Companies should always send letters of rejection to unsuccessful applicants so that they are clear about the status of their application.

REQUIREMENTS (n) require (v)

Requirements are the abilities, qualifications and experience that you must have for a particular job.

* Job requirements
* Fulfil the requirements of the post

> The requirements for this post include a university degree, three years' experience, and the ability to speak two foreign languages.

RÉSUMÉ (n)

A résumé is a written summary of your career up to now. See also CV.

 * A career résumé

> Candidates are invited to send a short career résumé together with their letter of application to the Recruitment Officer.

SALARY (n)

The salary is the money that you are paid for doing a job. A salary is usually paid monthly.

* The starting salary
* An attractive salary
* A competitive salary
* A salary proposal

> Companies do not always give the starting salary for a job in the job advertisement.
> Job advertisements often talk about an attractive or a competitive salary but do not give a precise figure.

SCREEN (v) screening (n)

When a company screens an application, it checks it to make sure that the candidate has the right qualifications for the job or is really the kind of person that the company wants to employ. See also SELECT.

* Initial screening
* Telephone screening

* The screening process

> Companies can get so many applications for certain jobs that some now use computers to do the initial screening.

SEARCH (v,n)

When a company or an agency carries out a search, it actively looks for and invites applications for a vacant post instead of waiting for candidates to apply in the normal way. See also EXECUTIVE SEARCH AGENCY, HEAD HUNT.

* Carry out a search
* A search consultant

> After carrying out a search, a head hunter will often recommend two or three names to its client.

SELECT (v) selection (n)

When a company selects a job applicant, it chooses the person who, in the opinion of the recruiter, is the best for the job. See also: SCREEN.

* Selection panel
* Selection procedure
* Selection process

> The selection process can take several weeks or even months for senior positions in large companies.

SHORTLIST (n,v)

When a company receives a lot of applications for a job, it usually draws up a shortlist of, say, six people, who go on to the next stage in the selection process.

* A shortlist of candidates
* A shortlisted candidate
* Draw up a shortlist

> Some companies ask all the shortlisted candidates to take part in a group role play or simulation together.

TAKE ON (v)

When a company takes on staff, it recruits new employees.

* Take on staff
* Take on new staff

> Companies which have to take on large numbers of new staff rapidly, need especially good programmes of initial training.

TEST (n,v) tester (n) testee (n)

A test is a short or informal examination to measure someone's ability or capacity in some area. A tester is someone who gives you a test. A testee is someone doing a test.
* An aptitude test
* A diagnostic test
* A handwriting test
* A personality test
* A psychometric test
* A test battery, a battery of tests

> A good psychometric test should measure - at least in part - certain main features of testees' personalities like how neurotic, how open and extrovert they are.

TESTIMONIAL (n)

A testimonial is a statement about a candidate's professional or personal qualities written by someone who knows him or her well, which the candidate sends to a company with his job application or CV.

> British employers ask for testimonials much less often today than they did thirty years ago.

TRACK RECORD (n ph)

Your track record is an informal measure of your career performance up to the present.

* A good track record
* A successful track record
* A proven track record

> When we say that applicants have a good or a successful or a proven track record, we mean that their professional performance has been good up to now.

VACANT (adj) vacancy(n)

A vacant position is a job with no-one to do it. A VACANCY is an empty position.

* Fill a vacancy
* A vacant position

> When a company has a vacancy, it aims to fill it by finding a replacement.

WORD OF MOUTH (adv phr) word-of-mouth (adj ph)

When you hear about a vacancy by word of mouth, you learn about it directly from a friend or acquaintance and not from an advertisement.

* Word-of-mouth recruitment

> Some companies never advertise vacant positions because so may people hear about them through word of mouth.

Chapter 4

Benefits

How many of these terms can you use?

ALLOWANCE   ASSURANCE   BACK PAY

  BONUS   SUBSIDISE   ACCIDENT BENEFIT

CHILDCARE FACILITIES   DEDUCTION

  CRECHE FACILITIES   WAGE

OVERTIME   ACROSS-THE-BOARD INCREASE

  FLEET   GOLDEN PARACHUTE

  GUARANTEE PAYROLL INCENTIVE

RATE   INCOME

  ASSISTED PASSAGE AVERAGE GOLDEN OFFERING

INDEMNITY CAFETERIA PLAN   CASH

  QUARTILE   DISCRETIONARY PAYMENT

  STOCK OPTION PLAN MERIT   PAY

   PERK LUMP SUM   EARN

BENEFIT SEVERANCE PAY   COMPENSATION

  PENSION   FRINGE BENEFITS

  COMMISSION EMOLUMENT   INCREMENT

PERFORMANCE-RELATED PAY   INDUCEMENT

  PIECE WORK DIFFERENTIAL VOUCHER

  GOLDEN HANDSHAKE PORTABLE REMUNERATION

   BASIC SCHEME   RATING

DRIFT   WEIGHTING CONTRIBUTION

  PROFIT-SHARING SCHEME INSURANCE

  SALARY   SERVICE AWARD

Exercise 1

Complete the following sentences by deciding which of the choices A, B, C or D fits best.

1. Normally we can work extra hours, but there has been no . . . . at all since demand for our products went down.

    A.   full time   B. extra time   C. overtime   D. part-time

2. She . . . . a good salary but she says that there is not enough interest in her job.

    A. wins   B. earns   C. gains   D. realizes

3. He asked to be paid in . . . . but we told him we always paid by cheque.

    A. money   B. notes   C. coins   D. cash

4. Business people in countries where there are high levels of taxation, say that there is no . . . . to work because the government takes a big proportion of any extra income.

    A. impulse   B. incentive   C. carrot   D. incense

5. It is true that our sales people get low basic pay but they can earn a lot of money in . . . .

    A. commission   B. revenue   C. income   D. compensation

6. When he retires, his . . . . should give him an income equal to about 75% of what he earns now.

    A. allowance   B. pension   C. benefit   D. profit

7. We all received a production . . . . for getting the big order finished on time.

A. commission   B. prize   C. bonus   D. reward

8. They offered me the job but I turned it down because the basic hourly . . . . was just not high enough.

A. tariff   B. piece   C. level   D. rate

Exercise 2

Below are six definitions. Give a word or phrase for each one.

1. Work which is paid per unit produced.

2. The group of directors which decides how the company's top managers should be paid.

3. A scheme which allows employees to choose between money and other benefits.

4. A plan which pays your family a sum of money when you die.

5. The large sum of money that senior employees can receive as a reward for good service when they leave a company.

6. A pay increase which is the same for everyone in the company.

Exercise 3

The verbs in the following sentences have got mixed up. Unscramble them.

1. We JOIN all our employees in cash in this company.

2. Every year the unions AWARD a wage claim and every year the management refuses it.

3. They won't receive any sickness benefit unless they UNDERTAKE it.

4. They don't TAKE OUT a bonus because they have not reached their sales targets.

5. The company has decided to QUALIFY FOR a salary review to rationalise the company's pay structure.

6. I want to SUBMIT an employee benefit plan to have proper medical and disability cover.

7. People PAY life assurance policies to provide money for their families if they die.

8. The management has decided to APPLY FOR a pay increase of 2% for the whole workforce.

ACROSS-THE-BOARD INCREASE (n ph)

When a company agrees to an across-the-board increase, all its employees get the same total or percentage increase in pay.

* Award an across-the-board increase
* Grant an across-the-board increase
* Negotiate an across-the-board increase

> The management did not agree to the demand for an across-the-board increase because it wanted to change the differentials between grades.

ALLOWANCE (n)

An allowance is extra pay for something special in your working conditions. See also WEIGHTING.

* An age allowance
* A car allowance
* A currency allowance
* An entertainment allowance
* A fixed allowance
* A generous allowance
* An overseas allowance

> Some senior staff in this company are paid an entertainment allowance but other categories, for example sales staff, have to claim expenses each time they entertain someone.

Cost-of-living allowance (n ph). You may get a cost-of-living allowance if you live in a part of the country where life is more expensive.

Hardship allowance (n ph). Your employer may pay you a hardship allowance if you have to live and work in a region or a country which is much more difficult to live in than your own.

Subsistence allowance (n ph). A subsistence allowance is a daily amount of money you receive from your company to buy food and accommodation when you are travelling away from home on company business.

ASSISTED PASSAGE (n)

You receive assisted passage when a company helps you to pay to move from one country to another.

> Employees taking up posts abroad will normally receive assisted passage to the new posting.

ASSURANCE (n) assure (v)

An assurance policy pays you a sum of money when something which is certain to happen does happen. INSURANCE is often used instead of ASSURANCE today. See also INSURANCE.

* An assurance policy
* Take out a life assurance policy
* Cancel an assurance policy

* A life assurance scheme
* Adopt a life assurance scheme

> The company decided to adopt a new life assurance scheme with lower premiums and more flexibility.

Life assurance policy (n ph)

A life assurance policy pays your family a sum of money when you die.

AVERAGE (adj)

The average of x numbers is the total of the numbers added together and then divided by x. For example, the average of 4, 6 and 11 is 7.(4 + 6 + 11 = 21 / 3 = 7.)

* Average earnings
* Average income
* Average wage, average wages
* On average

> If your income changes a lot from week to week or from month to month, it is important to know what your average earnings are.

BACK PAY (n ph)

Back pay is money which the company owes you for work which you did in the past and for which you have not been paid. See also Chapter 4: PAY.

> When the company found a mistake in the way it had calculated commission on sales for the previous year, some of the sales reps. received a large sum of money in back pay.

BASIC (adj)

Your basic pay is your standard salary or wage, not including any extra payments like bonuses, commission, overtime pay or other non-standard earnings.

* Basic income
* Basic pay
* Basic rate, basic pay rate
* Basic salary
* Basic wage
* Be on the basic rate
* Start at the basic rate

> In some companies where basic pay rates are low, employees may have the chance to earn more by working overtime.
> Sales people often have low basic pay but have the chance to earn more from commission on sales.
> When you start a new job, you are often on the basic rate to start with, but you go on to a higher rate later on.

BENEFIT (n, v)

1. Benefits are advantages, like, for example, a pension plan or a health insurance scheme, which you get from your company in addition to your basic wage or salary. See also COMPENSATION, REMUNERATION.

* A benefits package
* A generous benefits package

> The benefit packages of senior British managers can include a company car, a private health insurance policy, help with the cost of children's private education, and a share option plan.

Fringe benefits (n ph). Fringe benefits are other advantages offered to employees, usually managers, as well as their salary. A company car or help with housing are examples of fringe benefits.

Mix and match benefits (n ph). A company offers you a mix and match benefit plan when you can choose the balance of benefits which suits you best from a range of benefits on offer. See also: CAFETERIA PLAN.

Relocation benefits (n ph). A company pays you relocation benefits when it pays for some or all of what it costs you to move house.

2. Benefits are payments you get from an insurance scheme.

* Death benefit
* Dependents' benefit
* Disability benefit
* Family benefit
* Flexible retirement benefit
* Sickness benefit
* Join an employee benefit plan
* Receive sickness benefit
* Apply for sickness benefit

> If a company wants its employees to join an employee benefit plan, it is important to explain all the details to them clearly.

Accident benefit (n ph). Accident benefit is the money that an employer or an insurance company pays to you or to your family when you belong to an employee benefit plan and you have an accident which results in your death or permanent disability.

Employee benefit plan (n ph). An employee benefit plan is a plan that gives you insurance against accident, sickness, disability or death.

Unemployment benefit (n ph). Unemployment benefit is money you get from the government when you do not have a job.

BONUS (n)

A bonus is:
1. an extra payment made to an employee for special work, or

2. a present.

* A bonus scheme
* A bonus payment
* A cost-of-living bonus
* An expatriate bonus
* A productivity bonus
* A performance-related bonus
* A Christmas bonus
* Qualify for a bonus

> Some companies pay bonuses when the workforce breaks a productivity record.

Loyalty bonus (n ph). You get a loyalty bonus when the company pays you extra money for staying with the company for a certain period of time.

CAFETERIA PLAN (n ph)

A cafeteria plan allows employees to choose between money and other benefits.

* Implement a cafeteria plan

> Cafeteria plans are complicated and expensive to manage and so must be explained clearly to a company's staff in order to receive the maximum support.

CASH (n)

If you are paid in cash, you receive your wages in the form of coins and bank notes.

* Cash in hand
* Pay someone in cash
* Payment in cash

> It is more difficult for the tax authorities to know how much self-employed people earn when they are paid in cash.

CHILDCARE FACILITIES (n ph)

Childcare facilities are the services provided by the company or the State for looking after young children - usually of pre-school age - while parents are at work. See also CRECHE FACILITIES, PORTABLE.

> It can be very expensive for companies to provide childcare facilities for its employees, but the results - lower absenteeism, lower turnover and higher rates of women returning to work after maternity leave - can be very positive.

COMMISSION (n)

Sales people can be paid commission in relation to how much they sell. The commission is usually a percentage of the sale price.

> Successful sales representatives sometimes earn more than their bosses because of the amount of commission they earn.

COMPENSATION (n) compensate (v)

Compensation is pay. Your compensation package is the total of all the money and benefits that your employer gives you. See also BENEFIT, REMUNERATION, COMPENSATION (chapter 7).

* A compensation package
* A generous compensation package
* A compensation policy
* A compensation scheme
* A compensation survey
* A compensation system
* Compensation evaluation

> Some companies offer their employees complicated compensation packages including a large number of benefits while others prefer to offer just money.

CONTRIBUTION (n) contribute (v) contributor (n) contributory (adj)

When you contribute to an insurance scheme, you make regular payments into the scheme. The contribution is the sum of money that you pay.

* A contribution rate
* A contribution period
* Contribution-linked

> When overtime was cut at the factory, some employees found it difficult to pay their weekly contributions into the contributory pension scheme.

Contributory insurance scheme (n ph). A contributory insurance scheme or plan is one into which both the employer and the employee make payments.

Non-contributory insurance scheme (n ph). In a non-contributory insurance scheme or plan, only the employer makes payments to the scheme, not the employee.

CRECHE FACILITIES (n ph)

When a company provides crèche facilities, it pays for a room with equipment and trained personnel where employees can leave their pre-school age children during working hours. See also CHILDCARE FACILITIES, PORTABLE.

DEDUCTION (n)

A deduction is money taken away from your wages or salary before you receive it.

* An automatic deduction

> Deductions can include tax, social security and national insurance contributions and insurance premiums.

DIFFERENTIAL (n)

A differential is the difference in the rate of pay between two different kinds of work or between two pay grades.

* Wage differentials
* Maintain differentials
* Narrow differentials

> A company wage structure with few pay grades and few differentials is easier to manage than one with a large number of differentials.

Erode differentials (v ph). Differentials become eroded when the rates of pay of lower paid workers increase faster than the rates of pay of higher paid workers.

DISCRETIONARY PAYMENT (n ph)

Discretionary payments are ones which employers choose to make when there is no contractual obligation to do so.

> Good employers make discretionary payments from time to time to help employees in exceptional situations.

EARN (v) earnings (n)

The money that you earn is the money you get for your work. Your employer pays you your earnings for the work you have done. See also PAY, SALARY, WAGE.

* Average earnings
* Net earnings
* A net earnings calculation
* Increase earnings
* Earnings-related
* An earnings-related plan

> Companies often tell their employees that increased earnings are possible only through increased productivity.

EMOLUMENT (n)

Emolument is an old-fashioned word for a payment.

* The total emolument

> The total emolument of some senior managers can be many times greater than the income of the lowest paid employees in companies.

FLEET (n)

The company's fleet of cars is the collection of cars which it owns or leases for the use of its employees.

* Car fleet management

> Our new software allows us to manage all the cars in the fleet and their drivers by computer.

GOLDEN HANDSHAKE (n ph)

A golden handshake is a large amount of money paid to employees when they leave the company as a reward for good service.

> Golden handshakes are not popular with everybody since usually only senior managers receive them.

GOLDEN OFFERING (n ph)

When a company makes you a golden offering, it asks you to agree to take early retirement in exchange for an improved pension and/or other financial incentives.

> When one company takes over another, the new owners may make golden offerings to the old management as part of the restructuring of the company.

GOLDEN PARACHUTE (n ph)

A golden parachute is a guarantee of salary so that executives do not lose salary if their company is taken over by another.

> Golden parachutes are usually offered only to quite senior managers.

GUARANTEE (n, v) guaranteed (adj)

When your employer gives you a guarantee, he or she makes you a promise about something.

* An income guarantee
* A guaranteed minimum rate
* A guaranteed minimum wage
* A guaranteed annual minimum wage
* Make a guarantee
* Provide a guarantee
* Offer a guarantee

> Some large Japanese companies have traditionally provided a guarantee of employment even during periods of economic difficulty.

INCENTIVE (n)

An incentive is anything which encourages or motivates an employee to be more productive. See also INDUCEMENT.

* An incentives scheme
* A share incentive scheme
* An incentive bonus
* An incentive salary

* An incentive system
* An incentive wage
* A financial incentive
* A non-financial incentive
* Incentive pay
* Incentive travel
* Act as an incentive

> When tax rates are high, managers complain about not having enough incentives to work hard.

INCOME (n)

Your income is the money you get from your work, your pension or from investments.

* Annual income
* Average income
* Fixed income
* Gross income
* Net income
* Real income
* Taxable income
* Income tax
* Make a good income

> Retiring employees must normally expect some drop in income even if they have a very good pension plan.

Disposable income (n ph). Your disposable income is the money you have left to spend after tax, social security and health insurance payments are taken away.

INCREMENT (n) incremental (adj)

An increment is an automatic increase in your salary.

* An annual increment

> Annual increments are less common nowadays as more and more pay agreements are linked to performance and productivity.

INDEMNITY (n)

An indemnity is a payment made to compensate for something, often an unpredicted loss.

* End-of-career indemnity
* Redundancy indemnity

> If an employee has a fatal accident while at work, the company may pay an indemnity to the employee's family.

INDUCEMENT (n)

An inducement is something that encourages you to work more. See also INCENTIVE.

* A financial inducement
* A non-financial inducement

> Companies offer a range of inducements to personnel but it is not always easy to measure the return on investment in terms of increased productivity or sales.

INSURANCE (n) insure (v) insured (n) insurer (n)

An insurance policy pays you a sum of money when an accident which could happen does happen. The insured is the person covered by the insurance. See also ASSURANCE.

* Insurance cover
* An insurance claim
* An insurance policy
* Take out an insurance policy
* Be covered by insurance
* Cancel an insurance policy
* Accident insurance
* Health insurance
* Life insurance (or life assurance)
* Medical insurance

> In recent years, employee health insurance cover has become a major cost for companies in the United States.

Insurance claim (n ph). When you want to get money from an insurance scheme, you make a claim to the insurance company.

* Make an insurance claim

Insurance policy (n ph). An insurance policy is a contract between an insurance company and the insured person.

* Be covered by an insurance policy
* Take out an insurance policy
* An insurance policyholder

Insurance premium (n ph). The insurance premium is the amount of money you pay to be insured.

LUMP SUM (n ph)

A lump sum is an amount of money which is paid to an employee all at the same time rather than at regular intervals.

* A lump sum payment

> Some pension schemes pay both a lump sum on retirement and a monthly sum after that.

MERIT (n)

A merit raise is an American English term for a salary increase given to an employee for good individual performance.

* Merit pay
* A merit appraisal
* A merit award
* A merit increase
* A merit plan
* A merit raise
 * A merit rating

> Merit awards in the USA are more often made to white-collar managerial staff than to blue-collar employees.

OVERTIME (n)

When you do overtime, you work extra hours.

* Work overtime
* Overtime pay
* Paid overtime
* Unpaid overtime

> In some countries, for example in Norway and Sweden, there are strict controls on the amount of overtime that can be worked in many jobs.

PAY (n,v) paid (adj) payment (n)

Your pay is the money you get for doing your job. Your company pays you for doing your job and at certain times when you are not actually at work or are not able to work. See also BACK PAY, EARN, SALARY, WAGE.

* A pay structure
* A unified pay structure
* Basic pay
* Equal pay
* Holiday pay
* Maternity pay
* Sick pay
* Sick pay entitlement
* Take home pay
* Performance-related pay
* Pay increase
* Award a pay increase
* Pay rise
* Pay scale
* Highly paid
* The low paid

* Paid holiday
* Payment system

> More and more, pay increases are awarded only in exchange for higher productivity.

PAYROLL (n)

The company's payroll is 1. the list of its paid employees; 2. the money paid out by the company in salaries.

* Payroll software
* On the payroll

> The job of managing a company's payroll is made much easier by the use of specially designed computer software.

PENSION (n)

Your pension is the money you receive regularly from the government or from a company or private insurance scheme after your retirement. See also PORTABLE.

* A pension fund
* A pension plan
* An occupational pension
* A portable pension
* Pension adjustment
* Pension entitlement
* Pensionable age
* Reach pensionable age
* Draw a pension

> The quality of the pension plan you choose can make a big difference to the amount of money you receive after your retirement.

PERFORMANCE-RELATED PAY (n ph)

Performance-related pay is a system which links how much you earn to an assessment of how well you do your job. See also PERFORM, PERFORMANCE REVIEW, RATING DRIFT.

* A performance-related pay scheme

> One of the problems of performance-related pay is that, after a while, more and more people get the top bonus even though their performance has not been exceptionally good.

PERK (n)

A perk (short for "perquisite") is any kind of advantage which you receive from the company which is extra to the financial and non-financial benefits agreed in the terms of your employment.

* Enjoy a perk, enjoy perks

> The commonest perk among British executives is the company car.

PIECE WORK (n ph)

When you do piece work, you are paid per unit produced.

> Piece workers do not always have the same employment rights as other members of the workforce.

Piece rate (n ph). The piece rate is the money you get per unit produced when you do piece work.

* Piece rate working

PORTABLE (adj) portability (n)

Something which is portable is something which you can take with you from one company to another when you change your job. See also CHILDCARE FACILITIES, PENSION.

* A portable pension
* Portable childcare

> As job mobility increases, more and more people want to have portable pensions which they can take with them when they move from one company to another.

PROFIT-SHARING SCHEME (n)

A profit-sharing scheme is a company plan to share the company's profits with some or all of its employees.

> Profit-sharing schemes can be a way not only of increasing employees' incomes but also of motivating them and getting them to identify more with the company's future.

QUARTILE (n, adj)

In comparative salary tables, the whole range of salaries for a particular post is often divided into three quartiles: the lower quartile figure is the salary of someone 25% up from the bottom of the range; the median figure is for someone in the middle of the range; and the upper quartile figure is for 25% from the top of the range.

> In May 1993, the lower quartile basic salary of a German Personnel Director was higher than that of the higher quartile salary of a British Personnel Director.

RATE (n)

The rate of pay for a job is the amount of money paid per hour or per unit of production. See also RATE (chapter 2).

* The basic rate
* Start at the basic rate
* A pay rate
* A piecework rate
* An hourly rate

> When you start a new job with no previous experience, you usually start at the basic rate of pay.

Sick rate (n ph). The sick rate is the rate at which you are paid when you are absent from work because of illness.

RATING DRIFT (n ph)

Rating drift happens when the people responsible for making performance ratings of employees give too many of them the top rating so that they receive more money in a performance-related pay scheme. See also RATE, PERFORMANCE-RELATED PAY.

> One solution to the problem of rating drift may be to increase the number of ratings in the middle of the ratings range.

REMUNERATION (n)

Your remuneration is the total of all the financial and non-financial benefits that you receive from the company. See also BENEFIT, COMPENSATION.

* A remuneration package

> A manager's remuneration package can include not only salary but also a generous pension plan, a company car, an entertainment allowance and so on.

Remuneration committee (n ph). A remuneration committee is a committee of members of the Board of Directors of a company, often including non-executive directors (- members of the Board who are not full-time managers of the company), which decides the pay of the company's top managers.

SALARY (n)

Your salary is the money that the company pays you for doing a regular job. Salaries are usually paid monthly. See also EARN, PAY, WAGES.

* Initial salary
* Gross salary
* Net salary
* Starting salary
* A salary advance
* A salary payment
* A salary range
* A salary review
* Undertake a salary review
* A salary scale
* A salary structure

> White-collar workers tend to earn salaries while blue-collar workers tend to earn wages.

SCHEME (n)

A scheme is a plan, for example of the different kinds of benefits that a company proposes to its employees.

* A share option scheme
* A stock option scheme
* A share incentive scheme
* A pension scheme
* A sickness scheme

SERVICE AWARD (n ph)

A service award is a payment to an employee for having worked for the company for a certain period of time. See also SENIORITY and INCREMENT.

* Long service award

> We make a special service award for all employees who reach thirty years' service with the company.

SEVERANCE PAY (n)

If you lose your job with a company, you may receive severance pay as compensation for being made redundant.

* Severance pay
* Severance package
* Severance terms

> A manager's severance package might include not only a lump sum payment but also advice about how to get another job.

STOCK OPTION PLAN (n ph)

A stock option plan or STOCK OPTION SCHEME gives managers the right to buy a certain number of their company's shares at a fixed price during a stated period of time so that if the price of the shares rise, the shares will be worth more than the manager had to pay for them. Stockmoption plans are also known as SHARE OPTION PLANS or SHARE OPTION SCHEMES.

* Stock option plans are a way of encouraging managers to link their income to the company's performance but one piece of research shows that the main influence on the share price is the general economic situation rather than how well the manager works.

> Stock option plans can be criticised in the press when they help senior managers to increase their earnings in a way unrelated to the performance of the company.

SUBSIDISE (v) or subsidize (v), subsidy (n)

When a company subsidises the cost of something for its employees, it pays part of the cost for them.

* Subsidised accommodation
* Subsidised holidays
* Subsidised meals
* Subsidised transport

> Some companies buy property in seaside or ski resorts in order to be able to provide staff with subsidised holiday accommodation.
> Although many companies build canteens, not all of them are subsidised.

VOUCHER (n)

A voucher is a kind of ticket with a money value, provided or subsidised by the employer, which an employee can exchange for certain kinds of goods or services.

> Since there is no canteen, the company contributes half the cost of one luncheon voucher per working day so that employees can take their lunch in a nearby café or restaurant.

Luncheon voucher (n ph). A luncheon voucher is a ticket with a certain money value, paid for by the employer or by the employer and the employee together, which can be used to buy lunch in cafés and restaurants.

Merchandise voucher (n ph). A merchandise voucher can be exchanged for consumer goods in shops. They are also known as retail vouchers.

WAGE (n sing) wages (n pl)

A wage is the money that the company pays you for the work that you do. Wages are usually paid weekly. See also EARN, PAY, SALARY.

* A decent wage
* The basic wage
* The average wage
* The minimum wage
* A wage ceiling
* A wage claim
* Make a wage claim
* Submit a wage claim
* A wage earner
* A wage floor
* A wage freeze
* A wage hike
* A wage increase
* A retroactive wage increase
* A wage index
* A wage rate
* A wage scale
* A wage structure
* A wage table

> Does a minimum wage help the lower paid or does it stop job creation?

Wage slip (n ph)

Your wage slip is the piece of paper which you receive with your wages: details of your earnings are written on it. A wage slip is also known as a PAYSLIP.

WEIGHTING (n) weight (v)

A weighting is an extra payment which you receive, because, for example, you live in a place where the cost of living is higher. See also ALLOWANCE.

* A London weighting

> The union wanted an increase in the weighting because it said that the cost of living was much higher in the capital city.

Chapter 5

Training, Development and Appraisal

How many of these terms can you use?

ACCREDIT   RESKILLING   SIMULATION
        WORK SAMPLING   CONTINUING TRAINING
HIGH FLIER   ASSESSMENT   CAREER
        CASE   WORKSHADOWING
LEARNER-CENTRED TRAINING   COMPETENT   APPRAISE
        CASCADE   MATERIALS
BRUSH UP   FALSE BEGINNER   APPRAISAL
    COURSE   DAY RELEASE   DISTANCE LEARNING
        METHODOLOGY   EVALUATE   COACH
    FAST TRACK   FEEDBACK   ASSESS
    IN-COMPANY   CONTINUING EDUCATION   NEEDS
ANALYSIS   COUNSELLOR   PROTEGE
INDUCTION   INSTRUCT   APPRENTICE
    COMPETENCY   SELF DEVELOPMENT   LEARNING
    EVALUATION   IN-HOUSE   COUNSELLING
TRAINING   LEARNER TRAINING   MENTOR
    TRAINER   MULTI-SKILLING   TAILOR
        NEUROLINGUISTIC PROGRAMMING   OFF-THE-PEG
TRAINEE   PRE-EXPERIENCE   PROGRAMME
    RELEASE   FACILITATOR   IN-TRAY
EXERCISE   RESOURCES CENTRE   ROLE PLAY
    COUNSEL   VISUAL AID   SELF ESTEEM
    SEMINAR   MODULE   RETRAIN
SKILLS   ORIENTATION   PERFORMANCE REVIEW
    TRAIN   BEHAVIOUR   JOB ROTATION
        IN-SERVICE   VOCATIONAL   WORKSHOP

Exercise 1

Complete the following sentences by deciding which of the choices A, B, C or D fits best.

1. At the end of the course, we will ask you to fill in a detailed . . . . questionnaire so that we know what you thought about the quality of your training.

    A. evaluating   B. input   C. opinion   D. feedback

2. The course will take place . . . . so that you do not waste time travelling to another location.

    A. in-house   B. in-factory   C. in-office   D. in-building

3. All the course . . . . you receive can be placed in your file and used for future reference.

    A. data   B. materials   C. paper   D. brochures

4. His old job was computerised so now he is being . . . . so that he can operate the new technology.

    A. recycled   B. retrained   C. rehearsed   D. reformed

5. He had a very successful . . . . in marketing which he gave up to become an actor.

    A. track   B. career   C. flight   D. path

6.   We are very proud of the .... training which we give to new employees and which includes learning not only about the work but also about the organisation and culture of the company.

A. retraining   B. apprenticeship   C. induction   D. skills

7.   It is important to .... all personnel in how to operate the safety equipment.

A. instruct   B. form   C. facilitate   D. qualify

8.   We followed a very flexible course programme with choices between different .... on health and safety, benefits, assessment and recruitment.

A. items   B. parts   C. pieces   D. modules

Exercise 2

Complete each of the following sentences with one of the words or phrases from this chapter.

1.   At the beginning of the training course there were twelve c ....
p .... but by the end, there were only six.

2.   My company has put me on a d .... r ....
scheme so that I can go to the local college of further education every Friday to study for a better qualification.

3.   Although he used several kinds of v .... a ....
including slides and overhead transparencies, his presentation was not very interesting.

4. We learnt about health and safety during the training by doing a
    r . . . . p . . . . in which one of us took the
    part of the Safety Officer and the rest were employees on the shop floor.

5. The graduate recruits to the company are put on a j . . . .
    r . . . . programme which gives them the chance to work in
    four different departments over a two-year period.

6. Before the trainers decided the structure of the course, they carried out a
    detailed n . . . . a . . . . of all the trainees.

7. There was no local college which offered the course that I wanted to do so
    I joined a d . . . . l . . . . programme
    involving learning by TV, radio and telephone.

8. He spent several years training as an a . . . . and has now
    qualified as a master butcher.

Exercise 3

Complete each of the following sentences with one of the phrases from this
chapter.

1. My annual a . . . . i . . . . with my boss is
    next week so I have to think about my work last year and my objectives
    for next year.

2. Only a few people in our department will receive training this year
    because there have been big cuts in the t . . . .
    b . . . .

79

3. I felt that I was not developing in my job and unsure about which direction to take so I went to see a c . . . . c . . . . whose advice was very helpful.

4. Although we did a c . . . . s . . . . on exactly this kind of question at business school, I don't think our analysis then will be very helpful in solving this real life problem.

5. We believe that your education does not finish when you leave school or university. We try to provide a programme of c . . . . e . . . . which will enrich all our staff throughout their working lives.

6. You will understand how important we think training is when you see our specially designed and purpose-built t . . . . c . . . . where all our training now takes place.

7. We are planning to run an a . . . . c . . . . where we will appraise our managers from all over the world in the same way.

ACCREDIT (v) accreditation (n)

An accredited organisation is an organisation with an official power to decide, for example, who shall be a member of a professional group.

> British companies must have their quality assurance systems approved by an organisation accredited by the government before they can use an international quality standard logo.

APPRAISE (v) appraisal (n) appraiser (n) appraisee (n)

When you appraise a subordinate, you measure or evaluate that person's job performance. See also: ASSESS.

* An appraisal interview
* An appraisal system
* Performance appraisal
* Self appraisal

> Appraisal interviews have less chance of being successful if the manager and the employee do not communicate very often outside the interview.

Upward appraisal (n ph). Upward appraisal takes place when subordinates have the opportunity to assess the performance of superiors.

APPRENTICE (n,v) apprenticeship (n)

An apprentice is someone who works with a qualified person for a period of time, usually several years, in order to learn a particular skill.

* An apprenticeship scheme
* An apprentice mechanic, an apprentice electrician, etc.
* Run an apprenticeship scheme

> Some companies do not run apprenticeship schemes because they are afraid that the apprentices will leave when their apprenticeships have finished.

ASSESS (v) assessment (n) assessor (n)

When you assess something, you make a judgement about its quality. See APPRAISE.

* An assessment centre
* Run an assessment centre
* Staff assessment
* Carry out an assessment of
* Make an assessment of
* Make a rapid assessment
* Make a detailed assessment

> Supervisors involved in appraisal have to make regular assessments of the performance of subordinates.

BEHAVIOUR (n) behave (v)

Your behaviour is the way you act and react in different situations.

* A pattern of behaviour
* Change behaviour

> The objective of all training is to change employees' behaviour.

BRUSH UP (v)

You brush up your knowledge of a subject, for example of a language, when you do a training course or a course of self study to remind yourself of what you had forgotten.

* The company invested in a self access resources centre for employees to be able to brush up their languages.

CAREER (n)

Your career is the process of moving from one job to another with increasing money or responsibility or both during your professional life.

* A careers counsellor
* A career path
* Career counselling
* Career development
* Career management
* Career planning
* Career prospects
* Careers advice
* A careers advice centre
* Career-minded

> We do not want to recruit managers who put their careers before their families and their private lives.

Career break employee (n ph). Career break employees are people who leave their usual jobs for a while to do something different.

Careerist (n)

Careerists are ambitious people whose careers are very important to them.

CASCADE (n, v)

A cascade system of training is one where a company first trains senior managers who then use the same programme to train middle managers who in turn train their subordinates so that the training passes (cascades) down the line from top to bottom.

> Our company has now decided to reject cascade training in favour of taking mixed rank working groups in order to have an immediate impact on the whole team.

CASE (n)

A case is a (usually) detailed description of a business situation or business problem used in teaching business and professional subjects.

* Case analysis
* Case study
* The case method

> In case study, students read a report of a business situation and then present their analysis of it to the teacher.

Case building (n ph). Case building is when trainees themselves write their own cases rather than analyse cases presented by the teacher.

COACH (v,n) coaching (n)

When you coach someone, you teach them how to do something better. Coaches help sports people, in particular, to improve their performances. You can also receive coaching before an examination or to improve your job performance.

> Companies with strong human resources functions are now investing more and more time and effort in coaching their high fliers to develop the skills they need for top management positions.

Coaching approach (n ph). In what the Americans call the coaching approach, a manager who is going to change his job, coaches the person who is going to replace him until he or she is ready to take over.

COMPETENT (adj) competently (adv) competence (n: uncountable)

When you are competent at a job, you do it well because you have all the skills which you need for it. The opposite of competent is INCOMPETENT.

* Gross incompetence

> She does her job very competently and will probably be very successful.

COMPETENCY (n) competencies (n pl)

A competency is a mix of skills, attitudes and knowledge applied within a particular cultural context to achieve a specific objective. COMPETENCE and COMPETENCES can also be used to mean this.

* competency assessment
* competency based performance
* competency management

> Successful international managers, according to one PM consultant, possess both "doing" competences, like being able to act as an inter-cultural mediator; and "being" competences, like psychological maturity.

CONTINUING EDUCATION (n ph)

Continuing education is a policy of providing learning opportunities for people throughout their working lives. Continuing education is also known as ONGOING EDUCATION. See also CONTINUING TRAINING.

> The difference between continuing education and training is one of emphasis: education is concerned more with the general learning needs of the individual and training with the job-related learning needs of the individual.

CONTINUING TRAINING (n ph)

Continuing training is a policy of providing job-orientated training opportunities for people throughout their working lives. Continuing training is also known as ONGOING TRAINING. See also CONTINUING EDUCATION.

> In France, almost all companies over a certain minimum size provide continuing training opportunities for their employees.

COUNSEL (n,v) counsellor (n) counselling (n)

Counsel is advice. A counsellor is someone who gives advice professionally.

* A careers counsellor
* Bereavement counselling
* Career counselling
* Debt counselling
* Outplacement counselling
* Pre-retirement counselling

> Companies employ counsellors to listen to employees' problems and to give advice or offer help.

COURSE (n)

A course is a set of training lessons.

* An after-hours course
* A correspondence course
* A refresher course
* A short course
* A training course
* Course fees
* Follow a training course
* Go on a training course
* Run a course

> Companies should send their export sales personnel on language training courses to give them at least a basic knowledge of the language of the countries where they are trying to sell.

Course participant (n ph). A course participant is someone who follows a course.

Crash course (n ph). A crash course teaches you a lot about something in a short period of time.

Extensive course (n ph). In an extensive course, the lessons take place regularly on, say, a weekly basis, over a longer period of time. See also Intensive course.

In-plant course (n ph). An in-plant course takes place in the company, probably for people directly involved in the production process.

Intensive course (n ph). In an intensive course, all the lessons take place one after the other. A week's intensive course, for example, lasts full-time for one week. Intensive courses are also known as immersion courses. See also Extensive course.

DAY RELEASE (n ph)

A person on day release is officially absent from work for one day per week in order to go to a local school or college to study. See also RELEASE.

* A day release scheme
* Operate a day release scheme

> Companies which do not have their own training centres may operate day release schemes instead.

DISTANCE LEARNING (n ph)

Distance learning programmes are for people who cannot go to normal classes because the training centre is too far or because they do not have the time or because the classes are not at a convenient time.

> Distance learning programmes can use a variety of different supports including TV, radio, computers and the telephone.

EVALUATE (v) evaluation (n)

When you evaluate something, you measure how useful or effective it is.

* Job evaluation
* Performance evaluation
* Programme evaluation

> Good training organisations use evaluations to make improvements to future courses.

Course evaluation (n ph). At the end of a training course, the trainer often asks the trainees to evaluate the course they have followed by asking them questions or by asking them to fill in a questionnaire.

Student evaluation (n ph). A student evaluation can be:
1. an evaluation of a student by a trainer, or
2. an evaluation by a student of a course or of a trainer.

FACILITATOR (n) facilitate (v)

When you facilitate something, you make it easier for people to do. Facilitators are trainers who try to make it easier for their students to learn.

* A workshop facilitator

> Some trainers prefer to call themselves facilitators to underline the importance to them of helping trainees to learn.

FALSE BEGINNER (n ph)

False beginners are language learners who never knew very much of the language they are learning and have forgotten most of what they used to know.

> False beginners need to be given the confidence to communicate as much as they can in the language they are learning.

FAST TRACK (n ph, adj ph)

A fast track employee is someone who is expected to get rapid promotion to higher positions in the organisation. Fast track employees are also known as FAST STREAM employees. See also HIGH FLIER.

* On the fast track

> A fast track recruitment system selects people who the company thinks will merit rapid promotion to senior levels.

FEEDBACK (n)

When you ask people at the end of a training course or appraisal interview what they thought about the experience, you are asking them for their feedback.

* Positive feedback
* Negative feedback

> We send a detailed feedback questionnaire to all training course participants two weeks after the end of the course.

HIGH FLIER (n ph)

A high flier is a young manager who is expected to rise to a high position in the company. See also FAST TRACK.

> High fliers recruited to British companies are often put onto a special training programme which gives them experience in several different departments.

IN-COMPANY (adj ph)

In-company training is provided by the company itself rather than by an outside agency. See also IN-HOUSE, COURSE (in-plant).

* An in-company training course
* An in-company training operation
* An in-company training programme

> The advantage of in-company training operations is that the trainers know the company and its products well.

IN-HOUSE (adj ph)

An in-house training course is a course which takes place physically inside the company, not at an outside location like a hotel or conference centre. See also IN-COMPANY, COURSE (in-plant).

> Some companies prefer to provide in-house training facilities for their staff so that trainees do not lose time travelling to and from distant training centres.

IN-SERVICE (adj ph)

In-service training is given to people who already have jobs. See also PRE-EXPERIENCE.

> One kind of in-service training aims to keep workers' skills up to date with changing technology.

IN-TRAY EXERCISE (n ph)

An in-tray is the metal or plastic tray on your desk in which incoming documents are placed. In-tray exercises are used in training, recruitment and in assessment centres. In an in-tray exercise, you are given a number of documents - letters, memos, press cuttings, agendas, and so on, all relating to a professional problem or to the work of a particular manager - and a task to complete within a certain period of time. This kind of exercise is also known as an IN-BASKET EXERCISE.

> The candidates for the job were all given an in-tray exercise and two hours to read the documents and to prepare to say what action they would recommend.

INDUCTION (n)

Your induction period in a new job is the time that you spend being taught about it. See also ORIENTATION.

* Induction training

> The induction programme that we organise for new managers includes telling them a lot about the culture and objectives of the organisation.

INSTRUCT (v) instructor (n) instructional (adj) instruction (n)

When you instruct people, you teach them something practical, like how to operate a machine, in a formal and structured way.

> Safety rules are an essential component in any course of instruction in machine operation.

JOB (n)

See JOB (chapters 1 and 3)

Job enlargement (n ph). Job enlargement gives a job more variety or responsibility.

Job enrichment (n ph). A job enrichment plan aims to make the job more satisfying to the person doing it.

Job rotation (n ph). A job rotation programme moves trainee managers from one department to another over a period of months so that they get to know all the different parts of the business.

> Good job rotation plans are not standard programmes: they are adapted to the needs of individual trainee managers.

LEARNER TRAINING (n ph)

Learner training aims to help trainees become more effective learners and to take more responsibility for their learning by encouraging them to think about how they learn and about what learning strategies suit them best.

> We include a learner training component in all our training programmes because we think it helps to make the training more effective.

LEARNER-CENTRED TRAINING (n ph)

A learner-centred training programme is one which encourages the learner as far as possible to decide the objectives, content, methodology and pace of the programme. See also: TRAIN; Self-managed training.

> The objectives of a learner-centred approach are to achieve higher levels of motivation and retention through involving the learner much more in the learning process.

LEARNING (n) learn (v)

You learn something when you know or understand something that you did not know before. When trainers teach you, they hope you are learning what they are teaching you.

* A learning culture
* An individual learning style
* Learning by doing
* Flexible learning

> What teachers teach and what learners learn are often two quite different things.

Action learning (n ph). Action learning is a method of helping managers to develop their abilities by exposing them to real problems.

Open learning (n ph). Open learning is learning which takes place at a time, place and pace which suits you best.

Learning organisation (n ph). A learning organisation is a company which aims to make its employees able to adapt to permanent change.

MATERIALS (n)

Training materials are the books, video and audio cassettes, films, computer programmes and so on that you learn from during a training course. See also TAILOR.

* Materials development
* Materials design
* Tailor-made materials

> The design and writing of materials can sometimes be the most expensive part of a training course.

Self study materials (n ph)

Self study materials are materials which you can study on your own, without a trainer.

MENTOR (n) mentoring (n)

Mentors are experienced professional people who agree to help you with your professional development by meeting with you regularly, giving you advice and telling you what they have learnt about the job during their own careers. See also PROTEGE.

> Having a mentor can be a very useful way of learning about your job from a much more experienced person during the early stages of your career.

METHODOLOGY (n) methodological (adj) methodologically (adv)

The methodology of a training course is the way the content is taught.

> Good trainers adapt their methodology to suit the learning styles of the individuals they are training.

MODULE (n) modular (adj) modularisation (n)

A module is one part of a training programme. See also PROGRAMME.

> A training programme for personnel staff might contain modules on policy and planning, health and safety, benefits, and employee relations.

MULTI-SKILLING (n, v)

Multi-skilling is training individual employees and groups of employees to be able to perform a variety of different jobs.

> Multi-skilling the workforce goes hand in hand with the development of a team building approach to production.

NEEDS ANALYSIS (n ph)

The needs analysis is the stage before the training course begins when you question the trainees to find out what their training objectives and their needs are for the course that they are going to follow.

* Carry out a needs analysis
* A detailed needs analysis

> Once the needs analysis has been carried out, the training department can design the course and then write or collect together the training materials.

NEUROLINGUISTIC PROGRAMMING (n ph)

Neurolinguistic programming (often called NLP) is a training method which aims at improved performance in an activity by 1. analysing excellent performance and breaking it down into small components, and 2. encouraging trainees to understand how their thinking processes affect their performance.

> Neurolinguistic programming is interesting because, more than most other training methods and techniques on the market, it seems to help trainees to make definite improvements in their performance of particular skills.

OFF-THE-PEG (adj ph)

An off-the-peg training course is a course with a fixed content, not one designed to fit an individual trainee or group of trainees. See also TAILOR.

> Many training organisations advertise a range of off-the-peg courses with brief descriptions of the objectives, duration and content of each one.

ORIENTATION (n) orientate (v)

An orientation course or programme trains you to understand a new activity or to do a new job. See also INDUCTION.

> Some people still receive little or no orientation when they start a new job: this can lead to inefficiency and loss of time and money later.

PERFORMANCE REVIEW (n ph)

Performance reviews are spoken or written summaries of how well people do their jobs. See also APPRAISE.

> There should be a close link between an employee's performance review for the previous year and the objectives set for the following year.

PRE-EXPERIENCE (adj ph)

Pre-experience or pre-service training is the training people receive before they start a job. See also IN-SERVICE.

> There is much debate about the usefulness of the pre-service education given to future managers in business schools.

PROGRAMME (n, v) or **program** (US spelling)

A training programme is a complete training plan for an individual or a group. A programme might include several courses or modules.

* Follow a programme

> The aim of the company's range of training programmes is to increase the level of performance of the whole workforce.

PROTÉGÉ (n)

A protégé is the relatively inexperienced person who a mentor agrees to help with his or her professional development. See also MENTOR.

> The success of mentoring depends very much on how far a relationship of trust and respect can be established between the mentor and the protégé.

RELEASE (n, v)

If your company releases you for training, it agrees to let you go on a training course rather than go to work. See also DAY RELEASE, RELEASE (chapter 2).

* Paid release

> It can be difficult for a small firms to release individual members of staff for training because there is no-one to replace them while they are absent.

RESKILLING (n)

Reskilling is teaching people new skills.

> One principle of any company training programme should be to reskill employees whose current skills are out of date and no longer needed.

RESOURCES CENTRE (n ph)

The resources centre is the place where a company's training materials are kept.

> Our resources centre is used by in-company trainers and also by staff members following their own self study training programmes.

RETRAIN (v) retraining (n)

When you retrain, you learn how to do a new job.

* Retraining programme

> Retraining programmes are needed when, for example, a company buys new equipment which staff members do not know how to operate.

ROLE PLAY (n ph)

When you take part in a role play, you invent and take part in a short improvisation of a situation which will help you learn or understand something. See also SIMULATION.
* A role play exercise
* Do a role play
* Take part in a role play

> On our health and safety training course, we did role play in pairs with one us playing the roles of the safety officer and the others taking the part of someone caught breaking a safety rule.

SELF DEVELOPMENT (n ph)

Self development is an approach which encourages employees to take responsibility for their own learning and for choosing the best way to do it.

> A company can encourage self-development by providing its staff with portable training materials - books, video, audio cassettes and so on - that they can work on alone.

SELF ESTEEM (n ph)

People with high self esteem have a positive view of themselves.

* High self esteem
* Low self esteem

> Employees with high self esteem - people who feel OK about themselves - are more likely to make a positive contribution to the company.

SEMINAR (n)

A training seminar is a meeting led by a trainer or outside speaker. In management training seminars, the leader often does most of the talking. In others, for example university seminars where the number of participants may be smaller, the students have plenty of opportunity for questions and discussion.

* Lead a seminar

> Some management consultants give the same seminar all over the world so that thousands of managers have the chance to participate.

SIMULATION (n) simulate (v)

In a simulation, you invent and take part in a short improvised drama in which you play yourself, not someone else. See also ROLE PLAY.

> Simulations of meetings and negotiations followed by analysis and feedback, is one technique for improving people's abilities in these areas.

SKILLS (n pl)

Your skills are the abilities that you have to do different things.

* Develop skills
* Upgrade skills
* Communication skills
* Language skills
* Life skills
* Management skills
* Supervisory skills
* A skills shortage

> Managers must have good communication skills in order to be able to explain what they want to the people under them.

Core skills (n ph)

Core skills are the essential or basic skills which you need to do a job properly.

Inter-personal skills (n ph)

If you have good inter-personal skills, you are able to communicate successfully with a variety of people.

TAILOR (v)

When you tailor a training course, you design it to exactly fit the student's needs. Tailor-made training is also known as CUSTOMISED TRAINING. See also OFF-THE-PEG, MATERIALS.

* A tailored training course / training programme
* A tailor-made course / programme

> Before clients come to our specialised training centre, they first of all undergo a detailed needs analysis so that we can tailor the training precisely to their needs.

TRAIN (v) training (n) trainer (n) trainee (n)

When you train someone, you teach them how to do something quite specific.

* A training budget
* A training centre
* A training course
* A training department
* A training method
* A training pack, package
* A training policy
* A training programme
* A training provider
* A training session
* Do training

* Follow a training course
* Run a training course
* Undertake training
* Cross-cultural training
* In-house training
* On-the-job training
* Management training
* Performance-related training
* Supervisory training
* Training costs
* Training facilities
* Training measures
* Training needs
* Training needs assessment
* Training resources
* Training trainers
* Trainee potential

> Some of the most common kinds of training courses organised by companies are to improve language, computer and communication skills.

Self-managed training (n ph). A self-managed training programme is one you organise yourself without a trainer or with a trainer playing only a less important role in your training.

Outdoor training course (n ph). Outdoor training courses can be part of an outdoor management development programme.

Survival training course (n ph). A survival training course places the participants in an unfamiliar, difficult and possible dangerous situation - on a boat at sea or in difficult countryside - where they must work together to solve problems set by the trainer. These courses are also known as Outdoor training courses.

Training levy (n ph). A training levy is a tax on companies, so that they have to spend a certain proportion of, for example, profits or of the salaries budget, on training.

VISUAL AID (n ph)

A visual aid is a technical support involving pictures which you can use to help you to communicate your message to your audience in a presentation or in training. A transparency projected by an overhead projector is an example of a visual aid.

> Visual aids like transparencies are useful in presentations but you should not use them too much.

VOCATIONAL (adj) vocation (n)

Vocational training gives you the skills you need to do a particular job.

* Vocational qualification
* Vocational training
* Vocational guidance
* Pre-vocational training

> There is a general need to increase the number of young people with vocational qualifications in Western countries because the shortage of skills is growing.

WORK SAMPLING (n ph)

Work sampling is when you try different jobs in a company either to help you decide which job you would like to do or to help you know the company better.

> This company runs a work sampling scheme which enables teenagers in their last year at school to try out different jobs for a short period.

WORKSHADOWING (n)

Workshadowing is when you learn a job from someone by following them around and watching what they do over a period of time. Workshadowing is also known as SHADOWING.

> Workshadowing, like mentoring, is a new name for a very old induction and training technique.

WORKSHOP (n)

A workshop is a practical form of training session with a high level of participation.

* A workshop leader

> Workshops can involve participants doing a lot of activities in pairs and small groups and then reporting back their experiences to the whole group.

Chapter 6

Health and Safety

How many of these terms can you use?

HYGIENIC   ASBESTOS   DRUG ABUSE

INJURE   AGENT

ERGONOMICS   FIRST AID BOX

HAZARD   ACCIDENT   HEALTH AND SAFETY

INDUSTRIAL   CONTAMINATE

PREVENTIVE   MACHINE GUARD   INSPECT

PROTECTIVE CLOTHING   EMERGENCY

BULLY   FIRE   HARASS   ENFORCE

FIRST AID   HEALTH

FIRE EXTINGUISHER   LIABLE

MANUAL HANDLING   INCAPACITY

NEAR MISS   NEGLECT   SAFE

RISK ASSESSMENT   PROTECT

SEDENTARY   PASSIVE SMOKING   OCCUPATIONAL STRESS

REPETITIVE STRAIN INJURY

SAFETY PRECAUTIONS   WELFARE

VENTILATE   SCREEN

NEGLIGENCE   STRESS   WARNING

SECURITY   TIGHTEN SECURITY

MUSTER STATION   REHABILITATE

TOXIC   PROHIBIT   USER-FRIENDLY

VISUAL DISPLAY UNIT   OCCUPATIONAL

WORKING ENVIRONMENT

Exercise 1

Complete the following sentences by deciding which of the choices A, B, C or D fits best.

1. The works council has decided to . . . . smoking throughout the company except in specially designated areas as from next Monday.

    A. prohibit   B. veto   C. give up   D. disallow

2. The Safety Officer . . . . all the safety equipment regularly to make sure that it is in good working order.

    A. oversees   B. inspects   C. overlooks   D. investigates

3. We have reduced the number of . . . . in the factory so much that we are now very proud of our safety record.

    A. disasters   B. crashes   C. accidents   D. blows

4. It is a basic rule of . . . . to wash your hands several times per day.

    A. conduct   B. sanitation   C. behaviour   D. hygiene

5. I left the job because the long hours and difficult conditions put me under too much . . . .

    A. oppression   B. problem   C. stress   D. difficulty

6. Since we could not open the window, it was impossible to . . . . the office properly.

    A. cool   B. ventilate   C. expose   D. clear

7.   The new sign . . . . people that smoking in this area is dangerous.

     A. warns   B. requires   C. instructs   D. trains

Exercise 2

Provide another term to match the following definition:

1.   A piece of equipment which is comfortable, easy and convenient to use is called: u . . . . - f . . . .

2.   Another word for poisonous is: t . . . .

3.   Someone who has to breathe in someone else's cigarette smoke is a victim of: p . . . . s . . . .

4.   Women who receive unwelcome sexual remarks or advances from men are victims of: s . . . . h . . . .

5.   One material which we now know can cause cancer in people who work with it without proper protection is: a . . . .

6.   A piece of equipment which protects machine users from injury is a: m . . . . g . . . .

7.   If you know how to give simple medical treatment to someone who has had an accident, then you are probably qualified in: f . . . . a . . . .

Exercise 3

Complete each of the following sentences with one of the phrases from this chapter.

1. Since I got my new e . . . . d . . . . chair, I have had fewer backaches than before.

2. One worker was killed last year and this year we hope of course that there will be no f . . . . a . . . . at all.

3. It is vital for people to wear the right kind of p . . . . c . . . . in order to reduce the risk of injury while at work.

4. There is now a total s . . . . b . . . . in this building so if you want a cigarette you will have to go outside.

5. All construction workers must wear a s . . . . h . . . . at all times on building sites to reduce the risk of head injuries from falling objects.

6. We have a regular f . . . . d . . . . once a month when the alarm sounds and we all have to go downstairs into the car park.

7. Someone put a lighted cigarette in a waste paper basket and a small fire started but we were able to put it out easily using the office f . . . . e . . . .

ABUSE (n,v)

If you abuse alcohol or drugs, you use them in a way which is dangerous for your health.

* Alcohol abuse
* Drug abuse

> Millions of working days are lost every year in the industrialised world as a result of alcohol and drug abuse.

ACCIDENT (n) accidental (adj)

When someone has an accident, they hurt or injure themselves in some way. See also NEAR MISS.

* An industrial accident
* A serious accident
* An accident record
* An accident rate
* Accident benefit
* Accident insurance
* Accident prevention regulations
* Accident statistics
* An accidental death
* Cause an accident
* Prevent an accident
* Report an accident

> Almost 30% of fatal accidents in the industrial sector in Britain occur in the construction industry.

Accident log (n ph). The accident log is the company book in which details of all accidents are written.

Fatal accident (n ph). A fatal accident is an accident resulting in death.

AGENT (n)

An agent is a substance which can cause a chemical change or a reaction. Agents are usually dangerous and may need careful handling.

* A biological agent
* A chemical agent
* A physical agent
* Exposure to an agent

> British companies have to label all the chemical agents in their factories clearly so that people can see what to do after an accident.

Carcinogenic agent (n ph). A carcinogenic agent is an agent which can cause cancer.

ASBESTOS (n)

Asbestos is a material used in many products and processes, for example in fire protection materials. People who work in an environment where they breathe in particles of asbestos dust can get cancer.

* Asbestos levels, levels of asbestos, dangerous levels of asbestos
* Exposure to asbestos, exposed to asbestos.

> Removing asbestos from old buildings is an expensive and dangerous job which should be done by an expert.

BULLY (v, n)

A bully is someone who physically or mentally dominates another person or who causes another person physical or mental harm so as to cause unhappiness and stress to that person. See also HARASS.

* A workplace bully

> Workplace bullying is increasing and companies as well as schools need a policy on dealing with bullies.

CONTAMINATE (v) contamination (n)

When an agent contaminates a working area, it makes the office or factory dangerous from the health point of view. See also Chapter 6: AGENT.

* Contamination of the air

> The company closed off the plant to check that radiation had not contaminated the area.

EMERGENCY (n)

An emergency is a very dangerous situation where you need to take immediate action.

* An emergency exit
* An emergency procedure
* Emergency lighting
* In the event of an emergency

> In the event of an emergency, the alarm bell will sound and all employees must leave the building by the emergency exits as soon as possible.

ENFORCE (v) enforcement (n)

When you enforce a rule, you make sure that everyone follows the rule.

> Companies must ensure that all health and safety rules are enforced.

ERGONOMICS (n) ergonomist (n) ergonomical (adj)

Ergonomics is a part of engineering design. The aim of ergonomics is to make machines, processes and products as comfortable, convenient, safe and healthy as possible for the user.

* An ergonomic design
* Ergonomically designed

> Ergonomics aims to provide compatibility between the user, the environment and the equipment.

FIRE (n)

* A breakout of fire
* A fire alarm
* A fire certificate, issue a fire certificate
* A fire door
* A fire escape
* A fire extinguisher
* A fire safety notice
* Display a fire safety notice
* A fire warden
* Fire drill, a fire drill
* Fire practice, a fire practice
* Fire detection
* Fire fighting, fire fighting equipment
* Fire precautions
* Fire prevention, a fire prevention officer
* Fire safety

> All employees should take part in regular fire drills so that they know how to leave the building if there is a fire.

FIRST AID (n ph) first aider (n ph)

First aid is emergency medical treatment. A FIRST AIDER is someone who knows how to give simple medical treatment to an injured person after an accident.

* A first aid kit
* A first aid post
* A first aid room
* First aid treatment
* Administer first aid
* Receive first aid

> Even very minor injuries should receive immediate first aid.

First aid box (n ph). A first aid box is a box containing items for basic medical treatment like bandages, ointment, disinfectant and so on.

HARASS (v) harassment (n) harasser (n)

When someone harasses you, they annoy or worry you by causing trouble for you on repeated occasions. See also BULLY.

* Experience harassment
* Complain about harassment
* Suffer harassment
* A victim of harassment
* A harassment policy

Personal harrasment (n ph). Personal harassment is another term for bullying. See BULLY.

Sexual harassment (n ph). Employees suffer sexual harassment when a colleague makes unwelcome sexual remarks or behaves sexually towards them in an unwelcome way.

> Companies can help reduce sexual harassment by making female employees understand that complaints about sexual harassment will be dealt with sympathetically and by making it clear who will handle such complaints.

HAZARD (n) hazardous (adj)

A hazard is any kind of substance or equipment which can be dangerous in the workplace.

* A biological hazard
* A dust hazard
* A health hazard
* A maintenance hazard
* A skin hazard
* A welding hazard

> Many minor skin hazards can be avoided by wearing gloves while working.

HEALTH (n)

An employee who is in good health feels physically and mentally well.

* In good health
* In bad health
* A health check
* A regular health check
* A health risk, a risk to health
* Health protection
* Health surveillance

> Companies with their own medical departments often provide regular health checks for their employees.

HEALTH AND SAFETY (n ph)

Health and safety is the area of personnel work which is concerned with keeping employees physically and mentally well and protecting them from workplace hazards. See also WELFARE.

* A health and safety code
* A health and safety procedure
* A health and safety policy
* A health and safety regulation
* A health and safety requirement
* Health and safety enforcement
* Health and safety legislation
* Health and safety rights
* Occupational health and safety

> Companies with good health and safety policies often have lower than average staff turnover.

HYGIENIC (adj) hygiene (n)

A hygienic workplace is a clean workplace. An UNHYGIENIC workplace is a danger to workers' health.

* Rules of hygiene
* Observe the basic rules of hygiene
* Observe strict rules of hygiene
* Occupational hygiene

> It is essential for workers in the food industry to observe strict rules of hygiene.

INCAPACITY (n) incapacitate (v)

An incapacity is any kind of physical or mental condition which stops you from working.

* A temporary incapacity
* A permanent incapacity
* Temporarily incapacitated
* Permanently incapacitated

> The fall incapacitated him for several weeks but he was able to claim sickness benefit and did not lose too much money as a result of the accident.

INDUSTRIAL (adj)

INDUSTRIAL, in the context of health and safety, often means work-related. See also OCCUPATIONAL, INDUSTRIAL ACTION, INDUSTRIAL RELATIONS, etc.

* An industrial accident
* Industrial disease
* Industrial injury, an industrial injury
* Industrial medicine
* Industrial safety

> The best way to reduce the number of industrial injuries is by enforcing health and safety rules and by giving all employees health and safety training.

INJURE (v) injury (n)

When an employee is injured in an accident, he or she is physically hurt.

* A minor injury, minor injuries
* A serious injury, serious injuries, seriously injured
* Suffer a serious injury
* Sustain an injury
* Suffer light injuries

> Workers can suffer serious injuries if health and safety rules are not strictly observed.

INSPECT (v) inspection (n) inspector (n) inspectorate (n)

When you inspect something, you look at it in detail or check it formally to make sure that it is as it should be.

* A detailed inspection
* Make an inspection
* Carry out an inspection
* A health and safety inspector

> After someone reported a smell of gas in the main factory, the safety officer carried out a detailed inspection of all the equipment.

Spot inspection (n ph). A spot inspection is an inspection which no-one knows about in advance.

* Health and safety inspectors may make spot inspections to make sure that production workers have clean hands and are wearing the right clothing.

LIABLE (adj) liability (n)

Employers are liable when they are legally responsible for damage, loss or harm suffered by employees.

* Accept liability for
* Refuse liability for

> If a company refuses to accept liability for an employee's injuries, the employee may decide to take the claim to an industrial relations tribunal.

MACHINE GUARD (n ph) machinery guarding (n ph)

A machine guard protects the machine's user from injury.

> Fixed machine guards must be properly fitted and inspected regularly.

MANUAL HANDLING (n ph)

When factory goods are manually handled, they are picked up and moved about by employees, not by machines.

* Manual handling techniques
* Manually handle heavy loads

> Incorrect manual handling leads to thousands of back injuries every year.

MOB (v) mobbing (n)

An employee is mobbed or is a victim of mobbing when other employees deliberately exclude him or her or try to drive him or her out of the company. See also HARASS.

> Clear policies on mobbing and harassment can help to reduce these problems inside companies.

MUSTER STATION (n ph)

A muster station is a place in a building, or on a ship or oil platform where people must meet when the alarm sounds for an emergency.

NEAR MISS (adj ph, n ph)

A near miss accident is an accident which almost happens.

> The company has had no accidents at all this year although there have been one or two near misses, one of which could have been fatal.

NEGLECT (v) negligence (n)

If you neglect to do something, you fail to do something which you should have done.

* A case of negligence

> Companies which neglect to enforce health and safety may find that they are liable in cases of injury to employees during working hours.
> An employee who has been the victim of an industrial accident may claim compensation on the grounds of the employer's negligence.

OCCUPATIONAL (adj)

OCCUPATIONAL in the context of health and safety means job-related. See also OCCUPATION, INDUSTRIAL.

* An occupational disease
* An occupational disability
* An occupational hazard
* An occupational health service
* Occupational medecine

* Occupational safety
* Occupational stress

> Asbestos workers can suffer from a range of occupational diseases such as asbestosis and lung cancer.

PREVENTIVE (adj) preventative (adj) prevention (n) preventable (adj)

When you take preventive action, you take action to stop something from happening. PREVENTATIVE means the same as PREVENTIVE.

* Preventive measures, preventative measures
* Take preventive measures
* Preventive medicine
* Preventive health, preventative health
* Noise prevention

> The company's absenteeism and sickness records have improved since it started keep fit classes as part of its preventive health policy.

Preventive health policy (n ph). A preventive or preventative health policy is a company policy designed to keep employees in good health and to stop them from falling ill.

PROHIBIT (v) prohibition (n)

When something is prohibited it means you must not do it.

> In France, smoking is prohibited in many parts of a company building by law.

Prohibition sign (n ph). A prohibition sign is a sign which tells you that you must not do something.

PROTECT (v) protective (adj) protection (n) protector (n)

Something that protects you keeps you safe from injury.

* Protective clothing
* Protective equipment
* Protective headgear
* Protective materials
* Protective measures
* Take protective measures
* Personal protective equipment
* Eye protector
* Ear protector

> People who work near noisy machines should always wear ear protectors.

REHABILITATE (v) rehabilitation (n) rehabilitative (adj)

A company rehabilitates employees by helping them back to full-time employment after an accident.

107

> He will have to have a long period of rehabilitation after such a serious accident.

REPETITIVE STRAIN INJURY (n ph)

You can get repetitive strain injury if you have to use the same parts of the body to do the same thing again and again. Repetitive strain injury is often called RSI. See also INJURE.

> One example of RSI is the pain that typists and secretaries get in their wrists and arm muscles when they work for too long at the keyboard without proper breaks.

RISK ASSESSMENT (n ph)

Risk assessment involves making a list of workplace tasks and then measuring the degree of risk or danger involved in each one.

> Supporters of risk assessment say that if you can first of all identify the major hazards in the workplace, you can then go on to reduce the size and number of hazards which exist.

SAFE (adj, adv) safety (n)

A safe workplace is one where employees are properly protected from danger.

* Electrical safety
* Office safety
* A safety committee
* A safety officer
* Safety precautions
* Take safety precautions
* Safety measures
* Take adequate safety measures
* Safety procedures
* Inadequate safety procedures
* Respect safety procedures
* Safety records
* A good / bad safety record
* Safety regulations
* Call for tighter safety regulations
* Safety rules
* Enforce safety rules
* A safety representative

> A safety officer must carry out regular workplace inspections to check a range of features such as noise levels, first aid facilities, lighting, temperature and so on.
> Companies with active safety committees tend to have good safety records and fewer industrial accidents.

Safety helmet (n ph). A safety helmet is a kind of protective headware also known as a HARD HAT. It is usually compulsory to wear them on construction sites and oil platforms.

Safety sign (n ph). A safety sign is a sign in the workplace - often showing a symbol - which gives information, instructions or a warning to an employee.

SCREEN (n,v) screening (n)

When a doctor screens you, he or she checks your general physical condition. See also MEDICAL EXAMINATION, SCREEN (chapter 3).

* Health screening
* Health screening assessment
* Medical screening
* Screening for drug abuse
> Employees of French companies have to go for a medical screen once a year.
> We now have a computer programme which allows us to manage the health screening data of the whole workforce.

SECURITY (n) secure (adj)

If your company has good security, it means that it is well protected from people who may wish to enter the buildings in order to steal or to cause physical damage or some other kind of harm.

* Security arrangements
* Security measures
* Tight security
* Tighten security

> Security is especially important for companies which fear that competitors may try to steal industrial secrets.

SEDENTARY (adj)

People in sedentary jobs spend most of their time at work sitting down.

* A sedentary job
* A sedentary occupation
* Remain in a sedentary position

> People who remain in a sedentary position for long periods during the working day should make special efforts to take some physical exercise outside working hours or even to do exercises at their desks.

SMOKING (n)

* A smoking ban
* Impose a smoking ban
* A no-smoking policy
* A no-smoking zone

> Some companies impose a smoking ban throughout the whole workplace while others create smoking and no-smoking zones.

Designated smoking area (n ph). A designated smoking area is an area in a factory or offices where people may smoke: smoking anywhere else is forbidden.

Passive smoking (n ph). Someone who has to breathe in someone else's cigarette smoke is a victim of passive smoking.

STRESS (n) stressful (adj)

Someone suffering from stress has feelings of anxiety or of mental and physical discomfort. A difficult situation is likely to create feelings of stress.

* Relieve stress
* Stress relief
* Stress symptoms
* A stress-related illness
* Occupational stress
* Under a lot of stress

> Stress is a major problem in the workplace although it is difficult to measure.
> Stress can be caused, among other things, by bad work relationships, bad job design, a bad work environment and bad work conditions.

Chronic stress (n ph). Chronic stress is extreme or very serious stress.

TOXIC (adj) toxicity (n)

Toxic means poisonous. The toxicity of a chemical is its potential to cause harm.

* A toxic hazard
* Highly toxic

> All toxic substances used in the workplace should be clearly labelled with indications about how to handle and what to do in an emergency.

Toxic substance (n ph). A toxic substance is a solid, a liquid or a powder which is poisonous.

USER-FRIENDLY (adj) user-friendliness (n)

A user-friendly piece of equipment is comfortable, easy and convenient to use.

> The working lives of screen workers can be improved by giving them more user-friendly computers with larger screens and less complicated programmes.

VENTILATE (v) ventilation (n)

A ventilated room has a proper supply of fresh air, or air circulated by an air conditioning system.

* Well ventilated
* Poorly ventilated

> Poor ventilation in the workplace can lead to headaches and breathing problems among employees.

VISUAL DISPLAY UNIT (n ph)

The visual display unit (VDU) of a computer is the screen on which the user can read text or figures. Another term for machines with screens is DISPLAY SCREEN EQUIPMENT (DSE).

> Regular VDU users should get frequent breaks from working on the screen and should also get regular eye tests.

WARNING (n) warn (v)

A warning tells you to be very careful because something is dangerous. See also REPRIMAND.

* A warning sign

> The notice on cigarette packets in some countries warns smokers of the dangers of cancer.

WELFARE (n)

Your welfare is your general well-being.

* Welfare facilities
* Welfare provision
* A welfare policy
* Promote welfare

> Company welfare policies are usually concerned with improving physical working conditions, for example, washing, canteen and rest facilities but welfare is also about managing stress levels and looking after people in general.

WORKING ENVIRONMENT (n ph)

The working environment is the set of physical and psychological conditions which together define the situation in which an employee works.

> Companies can improve productivity and reduce staff turnover by improving the employees' working environment.

Chapter 7

Employee Relations

How many of these terms can you use?

ABSENTEEISM   BLACKLEG   AGENDA
BRANCH   CLOSED SHOP   CO-DETERMINATION
COMPENSATION   CONCILIATOR   DEADLOCK
ABSENT   INDUSTRIAL TRIBUNAL   DEAL
SHOP STEWARD   AMALGAMATE   BALLOT
ARBITRATE   DISPUTE   MOB
WORKS COUNCIL   RECOGNIZE   APPEAL
DEMARCATION   GRIEVANCE   DERECOGNIZE
EMPLOYEE PARTICIPATION   POACH   PICKET
EMPLOYEE RELATIONS   EMPLOYERS' ASSOCIATION
INDUSTRIAL ACTION   REPRIMAND   SETTLEMENT
JOINT CONSULTATION   LOCKOUT   SCAB
INDUSTRIAL RELATIONS   NEGOTIATE   NO-STRIKE AGREEMENT
NO-UNION AGREEMENT   DISCIPLINE   WHISTLEBLOWING
PARITY   TRADE UNION   UNION
WORK-TO-RULE   MISDEMEANOUR   RANK AND FILE
MEMBER   REINSTATE   RENEGE
BARGAIN   PARTY   HEARING
RESTRICTIVE PRACTICE   SINGLE UNION AGREEMENT
MEDIATOR   SEQUESTRATE   SUBSCRIPTION
ARBITRATION   SUPERVISORY BOARD   SUSPEND
VICTIMISE   WITHDRAWAL OF LABOUR   WORKER
DIRECTOR   STRIKE
DILUTION AGREEMENT   INTER-UNION DISPUTE

Exercise 1

Complete the following sentences by deciding which of the choices A, B, C or D fits best.

1. We must draw up an . . . . before tomorrow's meeting with the employees' representatives.

    A. action   B. order paper   C. agenda   D. list of points

2. He wasn't at work on Tuesday and Friday last week and now he is . . . . again today.

    A. absent   B. absented   C. out   D. unattended

3. We agreed to set up the factory here on condition that the workforce would be represented by a single . . . .

    A. trade association   B. employers' association   C. trades union
    D. employees' association

4. The pay . . . . went on for several days but the two sides were unable to reach agreement.

    A. discussing   B. talking   C. bargaining   D. threatening

5. Neither side in the industrial . . . . wanted to move from its original position.

    A. discussion   B. disagreement   C. discord   D. dispute

6. The talks finally broke down when the workforce said that they would . . . . if the management did not agree to a 5% pay increase.

    A. strike   B. hit   C. revolt   D. wildcat

7. Since the two sides could not agree, the management suggested that they call in an independent third . . . . to try to find a solution.

    A. side   B. party   C. person   D. man

Exercise 2

Provide terms which mean the same as the definition given below.

1. A secret vote, for example, to elect a union officer or to decide whether to take industrial action.

2. A person or group of people standing outside a factory or office to protest against something, to encourage other workers from joining a strike, or to discourage people from entering a building.

3. A formal criticism by an employer of an employee for not behaving in the way the employer expects.

4. A request to a higher court to change the judgement of a lower court.

5. This happens when one union tries to take members from another union.

6. A special court which has the power to make decisions in disputes between employees and employers.

7. Any form of protest to management about pay or conditions by an employee or a group of employees.

Exercise 3

Complete each of the following sentences with one of the phrases from this chapter.

1. We try hard to involve all our employees as much as possible and as a result we feel that we have a very good i . . . . r . . . . r . . . .

2. Although discussions broke off at one point, the two sides finally agreed to sit down again at the n . . . . t . . . .

3. However, the talks went badly and the union finally decided to b . . . . o . . . . the negotiations because they saw no reason to continue.

4. The industrial tribunal not only agreed that she had been wrongfully dismissed but also a . . . . her c . . . . for loss of earnings.

5. The company warned him that if he arrived late for work once more, they would take d . . . . a . . . . against him.

6. Our employee relations are so good that we have the lowest l . . . . of a . . . . in the area with very few people staying away from work without good reason.

ABSENT (adj) absence (n) absentee (n)

When you are absent from work, you stay away from work because, for example, you are ill. An absentee is someone who is away from work.

* Absent from work
* Absent owing to illness
* Absence analysis
* Absence monitoring
* Repeated absence from work

> When employees are absent, they should know who in the company to tell, when to do this and what information to give.

Absence without leave (n ph). Absence without leave is being away from work without permission.

ABSENTEEISM (n)

Absenteeism is the problem of frequent absence from work, often without a good reason.

* A low rate of absenteeism, a high rate of absenteeism
* A low level of absenteeism, a high level of absenteeism

> Any company with a high level of absenteeism should look very seriously at the reasons and take action to reduce it permanently.

AGENDA (n)

An agenda is a list of points to discuss at a meeting.

> It will be easier for negotiators to reach agreement if they can agree on the agenda first.

Draw up an agenda (v ph). To draw up an agenda is to write an agenda.

Circulate the agenda (v ph). To circulate the agenda is to send a copy of the agenda to all the participants in the meeting.

AMALGAMATE (v) amalgamation (n) amalgamated (adj)

When two or more unions amalgamate, they join together to become one single union.

APPEAL (n,v)

If you do not like the decision of a tribunal, you may decide to appeal to a higher court. An appeal is a request to a higher court to reconsider the judgement of a lower court. See: INDUSTRIAL TRIBUNAL.

* Hear an appeal
* Lodge an appeal
* A right of appeal

> You do not always have the right to appeal against the judgement of a tribunal, and if you do, you have to appeal within a certain period of time.

ARBITRATE (v) arbitration (n) arbitrator (n)

When a negotiation between an employer and a union breaks down, the two sides can agree to ask someone else - a third party - to arbitrate, that is, to try to bring the two sides to an agreement. This person is called the arbitrator. The arbitrator's decision is often a compromise between the positions of the two parties. See also CONCILIATOR, MEDIATOR.

* An arbitration award
* An independent arbitrator
* Compulsory arbitration
* Go to arbitration
* Refer a dispute to arbitration
* Resort to arbitration
* Submit a dispute to arbitration
* Take a dispute to arbitration
* Accept the arbitrator's ruling

> Two sides in a dispute normally resort to arbitration only if all other attempts at mediation and conciliation have failed.

Arbitration ruling (n ph). The arbitration ruling is the decision of the arbitrator.

* Reject the arbitrator's ruling

Binding arbitration (n ph). If both parties agree to binding arbitration, they cannot legally reject the arbitrator's decision.

Final offer arbitration (n ph). In final offer arbitration, the arbitrator must decide 100% for one party and against the other. He or she cannot compromise. This is also known as pendulum arbitration.

BALLOT (n,v)

A ballot is a secret vote organised by a union to allow its members, for example, to elect union officers, or to decide whether to go on strike. A union ballots its members when it wants their opinion on an important question.

* Ballot members
* Hold a ballot
* Organize a ballot
* A ballot paper
* A postal ballot
* A secret ballot

> In some countries, unions are obliged by law to hold a ballot before calling a strike.

BARGAIN (v) bargaining (n, adj)

Management and workers' representatives bargain when they have formal discussions in order to solve a problem or reach an agreement on, for example, pay or conditions. To bargain is to negotiate. See also: NEGOTIATE.

* A bargaining session
* A round of bargaining
* Central bargaining
* Centralised bargaining
* Joint bargaining
* Tough bargaining
* A tough bargaining position
* A weak bargaining position
* Industry-wide bargaining
* Productivity bargaining
* Engage in bargaining

> When unions and management bargain together, it is useful, first of all, to agree on an agenda.

Collective bargaining (n ph). Collective bargaining is a form of central negotiation - often at national level - between workers' representatives and management about wages and working conditions.

* A collective bargaining agreement
* A collective contract

BLACKLEG (n)

Blackleg is a word used by union supporters to describe someone who continues to work during a strike or who takes the job of someone on strike. See also SCAB.

* Blackleg labour

> The workers who refused to join the strike called by the union were called blacklegs by their striking colleagues.

BRANCH (n)

A branch is a local section of a trade union's organization.

* A local branch of a union, a local union branch
* A company branch of a union
* A local branch official

> In Britain, there are few members present at many union local branch meetings.

CLOSED SHOP (n ph)

In a closed shop, all the members of the workforce are unionized.

* A closed shop agreement

> If an employer agrees to a closed shop, he agrees to give certain jobs only to union members or to employ only union members in certain sections of the company.

CO-DETERMINATION (n)

Co-determination is the practice of management and employees working together to solve labour relations problems and cooperating in other areas of company business. See also EMPLOYEE PARTICIPATION and INDUSTRIAL DEMOCRACY.

> The new management of the company wants to develop a detailed co-determination policy with representatives of the employees.

COMPENSATION (n) compensate (v) compensatory (adj)

You receive compensation when a company pays you for something that you have lost or have had damaged. See also COMPENSATION (chapter 4).

* Compensation for loss of earnings
* Lump sum compensation
* Substantial compensation
* Award compensation
* Appeal for compensation
* Claim compensation
* Pay compensation

> An industrial tribunal can award an employee substantial compensation if it decides, for example, that a company was responsible for an employee's injuries because of inadequate safety procedures.

CONCILIATOR (n) conciliate (v) conciliation (n) conciliatory (adj)

A conciliator is usually a third party who tries to persuade the two parties in a negotiation to change their positions when there is a risk that the negotiation will break down. See also ARBITRATE, MEDIATOR.

* a conciliation board
* a conciliation committee
* conciliation proceedings
* call in a conciliator
* resort to a conciliator

> In a major dispute, a government may conciliate in order to try and avert a strike.

DEADLOCK (n, v)

When negotiations reach deadlock, the two sides in a dispute are unable to reach any kind of agreement.

* Break a deadlock
* Reach deadlock

> After a week of deadlock, the two sides at last agreed to submit the matter to arbitration.

DEAL (n)

A deal is an agreement.

* A pay deal
* A deal on pay and conditions

> One of the main jobs of a union is to negotiate deals on pay and conditions for their members.

DEMARCATION (n) demarcate (v)

Demarcation is the definition of a clear distinction between the responsibilities of one employee or group of employees and another.

* A demarcation dispute

> Since the arrival of teamworking practices in Britain, there are fewer demarcation disputes between unions about who should do what.

DERECOGNIZE (v) derecognition (n)

When a company derecognizes a union, it tells the union that it will no longer accept it as the organisation representing the employees for the purposes of negotiating on wages, health and safety, and so on.

> The more union membership fell in Britain in the 1980s, the easier it became for companies to derecognize unions.

DILUTION AGREEMENT (n ph)

A dilution agreement is one which allows unskilled labour to be used when skilled labour is unavailable.

> Dilution agreements are typical of the more flexible approach adopted by many unions in the 1990s.

DISCIPLINE (n,v) disciplinary (adj)

All members of organizations have to follow rules. Maintaining discipline means making sure that people in a company follow its rules. When employers discipline employees, they punish them in some way for not following the rules. See also REPRIMAND.

* A disciplinary procedure
* Disciplinary action
* Take disciplinary action
* Disciplinary rules
* Be the subject of disciplinary proceedings
* Maintain discipline

> The way a personnel manager handles disciplinary procedures can have a big influence on the whole organization.

Breach of discipline (n ph). There is a breach of discipline when an employee breaks a disciplinary rule.

DISPUTE (n,v)

A dispute is a disagreement, for example between an employer and a group of employees represented by their union.

* a pay dispute, a dispute over pay
* a demarcation dispute
* an industrial dispute
* a labour dispute

> A main objective of discussions between management and unions is to try to avoid industrial disputes.

EMPLOYEE PARTICIPATION (n)

Employee participation is a policy or philosophy of encouraging employees to play an active part in the affairs of the company. Employee participation is also known as INDUSTRIAL DEMOCRACY. See also CO-DETERMINATION.

* Achieve a high level of employee participation
* A low level of employee participation

> Some companies and unions working together, achieve a high level of employee participation in areas such as training policy, quality assurance and health and safety controls.

EMPLOYEE RELATIONS (n ph)

Employee relations are the relations between a company's management and its employees. See also INDUSTRIAL RELATIONS.

* Cultivate good employee relations

> A main objective of a personnel department is to develop and maintain good employee relations.

EMPLOYERS' ASSOCIATION (n ph)

An employers' association is a group representing employers in a certain area or from a certain industry. An employers' association may also be called an EMPLOYERS' ORGANISATION.

> In collective bargaining, union representatives may negotiate with representatives of the employers' association.

GRIEVANCE (n)

A grievance is a formal complaint. When employees are unhappy about some part of their work, they may decide to initiate a grievance.

* A genuine grievance
* A grievance committee
* A grievance procedure
* Grievance handling
* Initiate a grievance

> The personnel department has an important role to play in defining the company's grievance procedures.

Air a grievance (v ph). When you air a grievance, you talk about the thing that is making you unhappy.

Settle a grievance (v ph). When you settle a grievance, you find a way of solving the problem in a way that satisfies the employee who had the grievance.

HEARING (n)

A hearing is a session of a court or tribunal when the judge listens to what both sides have to say. See also INDUSTRIAL TRIBUNAL.

> A tribunal hearing should not make people feel nervous or frightened: it should be less formal than a normal court of law.

INDUSTRIAL ACTION (n ph)

When a group of employees decides to take industrial action, it decides on a way of protesting to the management about pay and / or conditions.

* Resort to industrial action
* Take industrial action

> Some examples of industrial action are the strike, the go slow, the work-to-rule and the overtime ban (a refusal to work overtime).

Secondary industrial action (n ph). Secondary industrial action happens when there are people involved in the industrial action who are not employees in the workplace where the dispute is taking place. See PICKET.

INDUSTRIAL RELATIONS (n ph)

Industrial relations are the relations between a company's management and its employees, in particular the unions representing the employees. See also EMPLOYEE RELATIONS.

* A good industrial relations record
* A poor industrial relations record

> The quality of the industrial relations in a company depend a lot on the quality of the communication between the management and the staff of the company.

INDUSTRIAL TRIBUNAL (n ph)

An industrial tribunal is a special court which has the power to make decisions in disputes between employers and em[employees. Industrial tribunals are also called INDUSTRIAL RELATIONS TRIBUNALS, INDUSTRIAL COURTS or LABOUR COURTS.

* Take a case to an industrial tribunal
* Appeal to an industrial tribunal

> If a tribunal decides that an employee has been unfairly dismissed, it may award that employee compensation.

Industrial tribunal hearing (n ph). A hearing at an industrial tribunal is a session of the court when a case is presented and discussed.

Industrial tribunal ruling (n ph). The ruling of an industrial relations tribunal is its decision in a particular case.

* A ruling in favour
* A ruling against

INTER-UNION DISPUTE (n ph)

An inter-union dispute or INTER-UNION CONFLICT is a disagreement between two or more unions. See also DEMARCATION.

* The negotiation of single-union agreements in Britain led at first to a number of iner-union disputes.

JOINT CONSULTATION (n ph)

Joint consultation takes place when channels exist for management and unions to discuss questions and problems frequently together.

> Joint consultation is an important form of internal communication in the workplace and can help to avoid many possible conflicts and problems.

LOCKOUT (n)

A lockout is when the management locks the doors of the factory during an industrial dispute in order to stop the workers getting in, and to try to force them to agree to the management's demands.

> It is rare today for an industrial dispute to become so bad that the management resorts to a lockout.

MEDIATOR (n) mediate (v) mediation (n)

A mediator in an industrial dispute is a third party who talks to both sides and tries to find things they can both agree about. See also ARBITRATE, CONCILIATOR.

> If all attempts at mediation fail, then the two parties may agree to send the dispute to arbitration.

MISDEMEANOUR (n)

If you commit a misdemeanour, you break one of the company's rules for employees.

* A minor misdemeanour
* A serious misdemeanour
* Commit a misdemeanour

> The management claimed that he had committed a serious misdemeanour and he is now the subject of disciplinary proceedings.

NEGOTIATE (v) negotiation (n) negotiator (n) negotiable (adj)

Management and workers' representatives negotiate when they have formal discussions in order to solve a problem or reach an agreement on, for example, pay or conditions. See also BARGAIN.

* Pay negotiation(s)
* Enter into negotiation with
* A tough negotiation
* A tough negotiator
* A strong negotiating position
* A weak negotiating position
* Sit down at the negotiating table
* Return to the negotiating table
* Break off negotiations
* A breakdown in negotiations

> When negotiations break down, the two sides sometimes agree to return to the negotiating table after the intervention of a mediator.

NO-STRIKE AGREEMENT (n ph)

When a union signs a no-strike agreement with a company's management, it agrees not to go on strike. A union can also sign a NO-STRIKE CLAUSE as part of a more general agreement.

* A no-strike agreement

> Unions usually try to negotiate better pay and conditions in return for signing a no-strike agreement.

NO-UNION AGREEMENT (n ph)

When the employees of a company sign a no-union agreement with the management, they agree not to join a trade union.

> Employees may agree to sign no-union agreements in exchange for guarantees on pay and job security.

PARITY (n)

When you achieve wage parity with another group of employees, you rise to the same wage level as that group.

* Achieve parity
* Gain parity
* Income parity
* Wage parity

> In spite of laws on equal opportunities in Britain, working women are still a long way from achieving parity with men in many occupations.

PARTY (n)

A party is a group of people involved in a negotiation or a dispute. In companies, the employer and the union are often the two parties or sides involved.

* A party to a dispute

> In some countries, a government arbitration service exists to mediate and to arbitrate between the different parties to a dispute.

Third party (n ph). When two parties cannot agree, they invite a third party to mediate or to arbitrate. The third party is someone who is not a member of either side in the dispute.

PICKET (n,v) picketing (n)

A picket is a person or a group of people who stand outside a factory or office to protest against something, to encourage other workers to join a strike or to discourage people from entering the company building.

* A picket line
* Cross a picket line

> Strikers may talk to people going in and out of the company to explain the reasons for their strike and to try to persuade them not to cross the picket line.

Flying picket (n ph). A flying picket is someone who travels from one picket line to another, perhaps several times in the same day.

Secondary picketing (n ph). Secondary picketing happens when the people picketing outside a company's building are not directly connected with the strike.

* Engage in secondary picketing

POACH (v)

A union poaches members when it takes members from another union.

> Poaching members is against the rules of the Trades Union Congress, the central union organisation in Britain.

RANK AND FILE MEMBER (n ph) rank and file membership (n ph)

A rank and file member of a union is an ordinary member, not an elected official or an officer.

> Although the shop stewards were in favour of industrial action, the rank and file membership were against it.

RECOGNIZE (v) or recognise (v) recognition (n).

When a company's management agrees to accept a union as the official organization representing some or all of the company's workforce, we say that the management recognizes the union.

* A recognized union
* Union recognition
* Seek recognition

> When a union has recruited a certain number of members in a company, it will seek recognition from the employer.

REINSTATE (v) reinstatement (n)

You are reinstated if you are sacked and then get your old job back, perhaps as a result of a court ruling or union pressure.

> The tribunal ruled that he had been wrongly dismissed and that he should be immediately reinstated.

RENEGE (v)

If you renege on an agreement, you refuse to keep to an agreement you previously made.

* Renege on an agreement
* Renege on a promise

> German unions claimed that the employers had reneged on an agreement to bring the wages of workers in the eastern part up to the same level as their colleagues in the western part within a certain period of time.

REPRIMAND (n, v)

When an employer reprimands an employee, he formally criticizes the employee for not behaving in the way that the employer expects. An oral reprimand is the same as a SPOKEN WARNING. See also DISCIPLINE.

* An oral reprimand
* A written reprimand
* Issue a reprimand

* An official reprimand
> An official oral or written reprimand can be a stage in the company's disciplinary procedure.

RESTRICTIVE PRACTICE (n ph)

A restrictive practice is a way of working of a group of employees, for example of union members, which gives them an unfair advantage over other employees or which stops other employees from working in an efficient and productive way.

> Although there are fewer restrictive practices in British industry than there were twenty years ago, there are still many restrictive practices in the professions.

SCAB (n)

A scab is an extremely strong term of abuse used by supporters of a union or of a particular industrial action against people who they think are against the union or the action. See also BLACKLEG.

> The workers who refused to join the strike called by the union were called scabs by their striking colleagues.

SEQUESTRATE (v) sequestration (n)

When a government sequestrates the funds of a union, the government takes away its money because it says it has broken the law.

>The union called on its members to vote for the right of protection against the sequestration of union funds and assets.

SETTLEMENT (n) settle (v).

A settlement is an agreement or a deal. See also DEAL.

* A lump sum settlement
* A pay settlement
* Reach a settlement
* Settle for

> Governments hope that the national average level of pay settlement will be lower than the rate of inflation.

Interim settlement (n ph). An interim settlement is one which is valid for a limited time. An interim settlement is designed to hold until a final settlement is reached.

SHOP STEWARD (n ph)

A shop steward is a member of a trade union and an employee of a company who is elected by the other members of the union in the company to represent them in day-to-day discussions and negotiations with the management.

> In a large company, a shop stewards' committee may exist to discuss all aspects of employee-management relations.

SINGLE UNION AGREEMENT (n ph)

When the management of a company wants to deal with only one union and a union agrees to this condition, the two sides can make a single union agreement. A single union agreement is also known as a SINGLE UNION DEAL.

* Enter into a single union agreement
> Japanese companies investing in Europe often prefer single union agreements.

STRIKE (n,v) striker (n)

The employees of a company go on strike when they stop working because they want better pay or conditions or because they want to protest to the management about something. A strike is a form of industrial action. See also WITHDRAWAL OF LABOUR.

* Take strike action
* Strike for
* Call a strike
* Come out on strike
* Be on strike
* Call the workforce out on strike
* Go on strike
* A strike ballot
* The right to strike

> In many countries in the world, workers cannot go on strike because strikes are illegal.

Official strike (n ph). An official strike is a strike which has the official support of the union.

Unofficial strike (n ph). An unofficial strike is a strike which does not have the official support of the union.

Sympathy strike (n ph). A group of workers strikes in sympathy when it takes strike action in support of another group who are protesting about something. We call this a form of sympathetic action.

Token strike (n ph). A token strike is a short strike, normally lasting just a few hours. The objective of a token strike is to show the strong feelings of the workers about an issue which may not directly concern the company.

Wildcat strike (n ph). A wildcat strike is an unofficial strike which happens suddenly.

Strike breaker (n ph). Unionists call a strike breaker a member of the workforce who refuses to go on strike with his colleagues and continues to work during the strike.

Avert a strike (v ph). When you avert a strike, you stop it from happening.

Call off a strike (v ph). When a union calls off a strike, it ends the strike by telling its members to go back to work.

SUBSCRIPTION (n) subscribe (v)

The subscription is the money that someone pays to be a member of a union. Some unions call the subscription DUES.

> Sometimes, union members pay a proportion of their income in subscription fees.

SUPERVISORY BOARD (n ph)

A supervisory board is a joint management committee whose members come from management and from representatives of the employees.

> In Germany, the supervisory board appoints the executive board which is responsible for the overall running of the company; and the employee representatives on the supervisory board appoint the company's labour director.

SUSPEND (v) suspension (n)

When an employer suspends an employee, the employee may not continue working although he or she has not been dismissed.

* Suspended from duty
* Suspended on full pay
* Suspended without pay
* Suspension pending disciplinary procedure

> Suspension from duty is a temporary status which may result in reinstatement or dismissal.

TRADE UNION (n) or trades union (n) trade unionist (n)

A trade union is an organization of workers which exists to protect and promote the interests of its members and which represents them in discussions and negotiations with management. A trade union is often called simply a UNION. See also UNION.

* A trade union leader
* A trade union officer
* A trade union official, a full-time trade union official, a part-time trade union official.
* A trade union confederation

> Unions are concerned about falling membership which means less income and less power.

UNION (n) unionize (v).

A union is the same as a trade union. To unionize is to encourage employees to join a union. See also TRADE UNION.

Craft union (n ph). A craft union's members all do the same kind of skilled job. An electricians' union is an example of a crafts union.

General union (n ph). A general union has members who do a variety of different jobs. These unions are generally organized into sections representing different occupational groups.

Super union (n ph). In Britain, a super union is a very large union, often the result of two or more already large unions joining together.

VICTIMISE (v) victim (n) victimisation (n)

If you are being victimised, you are being unfairly treated by your employer or by another employee or group of employees in your company.

> After disagreeing with the company's new policies, he began to feel that he was not being treated in the same way as his colleagues and that he was being victimised.

WHISTLEBLOWING (n)

When employees blow the whistle at work, they draw attention to something which they think is wrong in the workplace.

* Blow the whistle on

> Whistleblowing in the UK is most often about fraud and corruption and also about health and safety matters.

WITHDRAWAL OF LABOUR (n ph) withdraw labour (v ph)

A withdrawal of labour is a strike. See also STRIKE.

> When the union withdrew its labour, the management withdrew its pay offer.

WORK-TO-RULE (n) work to rule (v)

When employees follow a work-to-rule, they do only what they have to do according to the conditions of employment and no more. They therefore work more slowly and produce less. A GO SLOW is similar to a work-to-rule.

> The union members voted to work to rule in answer to the employer's pay offer.

WORKER DIRECTOR (n ph)

A worker director is a representative of the employees who sits on the Management Board of the company.

> Worker directors are common in Germany because of that country's co-determination laws.

WORKS COUNCIL (n)

A works council is a committee of employees' representatives and management.

> The powers and activities of works councils can vary a great deal: some have limited powers, for example, to manage the company's training programme; others discuss company finance and strategic questions.

APPENDIX

Some Abbreviations in Personnel

CPD	Continuing Professional Development
CPIS	Computerised Personnel Information System
CV	Curriculum Vitae
DSE	Display Screen Equipment
EAP	Employee Assistance Programme
ESOP	Employee Share Option Scheme
EU	European Union
HR	Human Resources
HRD	Human Resources Development
IPD	Institute of Personnel and Development (GB)
LIFO	Last In, First Out
MD	Management Development
NLP	Neurolinguistic Programming
NVQ	National Vocational Qualification (GB)
PAQ	Position Analysis Questionnaire
PBR	Payment By Results
PRP	Performance-Related Pay / Profit-Related Pay
SMP	Statutory Maternity Pay
TEC	Training and Entreprise Council (GB)
TCN	Third Country National
VDU	Visual Display Unit
VQ	Vocational Qualification

EXERCISE KEY

CHAPTER 1: BASIC TERMS AND WORKING CONDITIONS

Exercise 1

1. B: contract
2. A: duties
3. D. employees
4. C. job
5. A. overtime
6. D. pilot
7. B. shift
8. A. turnover

Exercise 2

1. day off
2. flexitime
3. holiday
4. superior
5. telework / teleworking / telecommuting
6. manual
7. part-time
8. skilled

Exercise 3

1. call in a consultant
2. gone on sick leave
3. bottom grade / top grade
4. management development
5. full employment
6. working hours

CHAPTER 2: PHILOSOPHY, POLICY AND PLANNING

Exercise 1

1. C: casual workers
2. B: promote
3. A: dismiss
4. B: lay off
5. D: goals
6. C: notice
7. A: overstaffed
8. C: relocate

Exercise 2

Downsizing the workforce is a major part of this company's rationalisation programme. Our **goal** is a 10% reduction in the workforce in the next two years. We think that most of this reduction can be achieved through **natural wastage**: a number of our older staff are coming up to **retirement** age and others may be interested in taking **early retirement**. We hope that only a few people will actually be made **redundant**. All these people will be given extensive **outplacement counselling**.

Exercise 3

Two years ago, when we became an **equal opportunities** employer, we took a long hard look at the way women were treated in the company and decided that we needed to make a lot of changes. Not enough women were getting **promoted** to the top jobs: there was a **glass ceiling** stopping women from being appointed to the most senior positions. So we decided to take **affirmative action** to improve the situation. We recruited more women. Our **positive action** training programme helped women to improve their skills. We even changed the language we used and started to talk about overstaffing rather than **overmanning** . We still have a long way to go but we have definitely made progress.

CHAPTER 3: RECRUITMENT AND SELECTION

Exercise 1

1. B. interview
2. A. reject
3. D. apply
4. A. appoint
5. A. recruit
6. B. vacant
7. D. candidate
8. C. select

Exercise 2

1. shortlist
2. confidential
3. advertise
4. CV
5. graduate
6. track record
7. medical examination
8. qualifications

Exercise 3

When a company decides to fill a **vacant** position, the first thing it may do is to **advertise** the post internally. It will invite **applications** from all **qualified** personnel: in some companies the applicants will have to **complete** a form, while in others they will have to write a letter and send this together with a **curriculum vitae** to the person in charge of **recruitment.**

Sometimes there are not enough good internal **candidates** and then the company may **advertise** in the national or specialised press. Once a good number of **applications** have been received, the company draws up a **shortlist** of two or three. These are invited to the company for **interview.**

This stage may last a few minutes or several days. The **applicants** may have to answer questions from one person or from a **panel** of several **interviewers.** They may learn the result of the **interview** straight away or only after several days or even weeks. The company may want time to ask for **references** .

Finally the company will make the decision to accept one **candidate** and to **reject** the others. Of course it is important for the company to make the right decision: mistakes can be costly!

CHAPTER 4: BENEFITS

Exercise 1

1. C. overtime
2. B. earns
3. D. cash
4. B. incentive
5. A. commission
6. B. pension
7. C. bonus
8. D. rate

Exercise 2

1. piece work
2. remuneration committee
3. cafeteria plan
4. life assurance
5. golden handshake
6. across-the-board increase

Exercise 3

1. We PAY all our employees in cash in this company.
2. Every year the unions SUBMIT a wage claim and every year the management refuses it.
3. They won't receive any sickness benefit unless they APPLY FOR it.

4. They don't QUALIFY FOR a bonus because they have not reached their sales targets.
5. The company has decided to UNDERTAKE a salary review to rationalise the company's pay structure.
6. I want to JOIN an employee benefit plan to have proper medical and disability cover.
7. People TAKE OUT life assurance policies to provide money for their families if they die.
8. The management has decided to AWARD a pay increase of 2% for the whole workforce.

CHAPTER 5: TRAINING, DEVELOPMENT AND APPRAISAL

Exercise 1

1. D: feedback
2. A: in-house
3. B: materials
4. B: retrained
5. B: career
6. C: induction
7. A: instruct
8. D: modules

Exercise 2

1. course participants
2. day release
3. visual aid
4. role play
5. job rotation
6. needs analysis
7. distance learning
8. apprentice

Exercise 3

1. assessment / appraisal interview
2. training budget
3. careers counsellor
4. case study
5. continuing education
6. training centre
7. assessment centre

CHAPTER 6: HEALTH AND SAFETY

Exercise 1

1. A: prohibit
2. B. inspects
3. C. accidents
4. D: hygiene
5. C: stress
6. B: ventilate
7. A: warns

Exercise 2

1. user-friendly
2. toxic
3. passive smoking
4. sexual harassment
5. asbestos
6. machine guard
7. first aid

Exercise 3

1. ergonomically designed
2. fatal accidents
3. protective clothing

4. smoking ban
5. safety helmet
6. fire drill
7. fire extinguisher

CHAPTER 7: EMPLOYEE RELATIONS

Exercise 1

1. C: agenda
2. A: absent
3. C: trades union
4. C: bargaining
5. D: dispute
6. A: strike
7. B: party

Exercise 2

1. ballot
2. picket
3. reprimand
4. appeal
5. poach
6. industrial tribunal
7. industrial action

Exercise 3

1. industrial relations record
2. negotiating table
3. break off
4. awarded .... compensation
5. disciplinary action
6. level of absenteeism

INDEX

Notes

1. Main entries in the book are listed in capital letters, followed by the page number. For example:

ABSENT   116

2. A term included in the definition of a main entry is listed as follows:

APPLICANT. See APPLY.

3. Collocations with definitions are listed in small letters. For example:

Agent, carcinogenic   100

4. Collocations are usually listed straight after the main entries which they follow in the book.